Just Us or Justice?

Just Us or Justice?

Moving toward a Pan-Methodist Theology

F. Douglas Powe Jr.

Abingdon Press
Nashville

JUST US OR JUSTICE?
MOVING TOWARD A PAN-METHODIST THEOLOGY

This book is printed on acid-free paper.

Library of Congress Cataloging-in-Publication Data

Powe, F. Douglas.
Just us or justice? : moving toward a pan-Methodist theology / F. Douglas Powe, Jr.
p. cm.
Includes bibliographical references.
ISBN 978-0-687-46553-8 (pbk. : alk. paper)
1. Justice—Religious aspects—Christianity. 2. Methodist Church—Doctrines. 3. Black theology.
I. Title.
BR115.J8P69 2009
230'.7—dc22

2008036676

Excerpts from James H. Cone, *A Black Theology of Liberation: Twentieth Anniversary Edition* (Maryknoll, N.Y.: Orbis Books, 1990), J. Deotis Roberts, *Liberation and Reconciliation: A Black Theology* (Maryknoll, N.Y.: Orbis Books, 1994), and Delores S. Williams, *Sisters in the Wilderness: The Challenge of Womanist God-talk* (Maryknoll, N.Y.: Orbis Books, 1993) used by permission.

Excerpts from Catherine Keller, "Salvation Flows: Eschatology for a Feminist Wesleyanism," in *Quarterly Review* (winter 2003) used by permission.

Excerpts from C. Eric Lincoln and Lawrence H. Mamiya, "The Religious Dimension," in *The Black Church in the African American Experience*, pp. 1–19. Copyright, 1990, Duke University Press. All rights reserved. Used by permission of the publisher.

Excerpts from Randy L. Maddox, *Responsible Grace: John Wesley's Practical Theology* (Nashville: Kingswood Books, 1994) and Theodore Runyon, *The New Creation: John Wesley's Theology Today* (Nashville: Abingdon Press, 1998) used by permission.

09 10 11 12 13 14 15 16 17 18—10 9 8 7 6 5 4 3 2 1

MANUFACTURED IN THE UNITED STATES OF AMERICA

To my parents, Frederick D. Powe Sr. and Betty L. Powe,

with love and appreciation

Contents

Acknowledgments

I want to thank Fred Allen for his guidance on this project. I want to give a very special thanks to Sherry Wright, who edited and offered invaluable insights for every chapter in the book. I also want to thank H. Henry Knight III, Nancy R. Howell, and Angela Sims for reading various parts of the manuscript. Thank you to Amy Slater for following up on library leads. A special thanks goes to Jeff Jaekley, who helped with most of the detailed work on the manuscript. I also want to recognize John Oyler at the Saint Paul School of Theology library for securing resources from around the country and helping me track down material at the school.

INTRODUCTION

"The more things change the more they stay the same" is a quotation that continues to describe the Methodist theological landscape. In the past forty years a resurgence of Wesleyan theology has occurred in Methodism. During this same time African American theology (I will use this term instead of "black liberation theology" because it is more inclusive of womanist voices) has become a fixture on the theological landscape. Specifically, an African American theological perspective has developed that relies heavily upon thinkers from the broader Methodist tradition.[1] Unfortunately, these two theological perspectives developed along parallel lines without intersecting in an explicit manner.

By intersection, I mean moving toward a Pan-Methodist theological perspective that integrates African American and Wesleyan theologies, while maintaining the integrity of both.[2] Some African Americans in the traditional African Methodist denominations (African Methodist Episcopal Church, African Methodist Episcopal Zion Church, and Christian Methodist Church), however, will resist the intersection I am suggesting because it "feels" like a subtle form of assimilation. Some Euro-Americans in The United Methodist Church will resist the intersection I am suggesting because it "feels" like forced integration. My goal is to resist moving toward either assimilation or integration and to develop intersections illuminating a true Pan-Methodist perspective.

Maintaining the integrity of these two perspectives does not mean a watered-down theology that creates one more polite conversation. Both perspectives must be challenged in those areas where preserving the status quo means theological stagnation. For instance, both African American and Wesleyan theologies make claims concerning justice issues (for example, racism, sexism, classism, and so on) but have not developed integrated responses to these matters. Is it because they are so different that no points of connection exist? Or is it because little effort is made to integrate the thinking of these two perspectives? Moving toward a Pan-Methodist theological approach is an effort to construct an intersection between African American and Wesleyan theologies that no longer buys into just-us concerns and offers new insights into justice-related issues through a soteriological lens.

Theologically this means focusing on how love and justice relate concretely, and how God relates to love and justice for the neighbor. This is important because many Wesleyan theologians argue that God defines the relationship between love and justice. Most African American theologians agree that God defines the relationship between love and justice, but they are often suspicious of Eurocentric interpretations regarding the relationship between the two. How then can we really listen to and be guided by God and not by culturally encouraged ignorance or cultural assumptions? How is an epistemology of the spirit related to the epistemological perspective of the disenfranchised? These questions guide this project in an effort to move toward a Pan-Methodist theology.

Just-us

Why is there no explicit intersection between African American and Wesleyan theologies, especially in responding to certain justice issues? I believe the problem is a snare called "just-us,"[3] into which many groups and communities fall. By just-us I mean seeking what is right or good for one's own community, yet remaining blind to a vision of justice that includes the broader community. For example, African American theology has not seriously studied John Wesley's stance against slavery or his work with the disenfranchised. Similarly, Wesleyan theologians have mostly ignored the insights of African American theology when it comes to a constructive political analysis of certain injustices. Both sides perceive justice from a particular vantage point that focuses on just-us (just our community).

How did we get to this point of just-us? There are several ways this question can be answered. In part, I believe our current theological situation of just-us within Methodism was caused by slavery and the resulting separation of some blacks from the mother denomination. The three major splinters separating the traditional African American Methodist denominations from what is now The United Methodist Church (UMC) were The African Methodist Episcopal Church (AME), The African Methodist Episcopal Zion Church (AMEZ), and The Colored (now Christian) Methodist Episcopal Church (CME).

These splits highlight theological differences that are still embedded in the ethos of their representative communities today. For example, embedded within the ethos of traditional African American denominations is an ideal of liberation from oppressive Euro-American structures. Breaking away from the predominantly Euro-American Methodist Episcopal Church (MEC) and Methodist Episcopal Church South (MEC, South) allowed the traditional African American Methodist denominations to determine their own destiny. It was after not being allowed to pray at the altar at Saint George's Methodist Church that Richard Allen resolved to begin a black church in Philadelphia, which eventually led to the AME Church.[4]

The history of splinters between Methodist groups makes it difficult to develop intersections because both sides are comfortable on their side of the fence. The challenge this creates is it perpetuates the notion of just-us resulting from the different splinters. On the side of the traditional African American denominations just-us is perpetuated because of the memory of oppression and a continuing suspicion of Euro-American theological intentions. On the side of Euro-American Methodists just-us is perpetuated because it seems there is no effort to move forward from the past. Both sides persist in constructing their theological perspectives on parallel tracks, disregarding the deeper structural issues of just-us.

Many African Americans in the academy still experience this attitude of superiority and question whether some Euro-American scholars are willing to seriously engage black and womanist theological thought. In a plenary address at the American Academy of Religion in Denver (2002) James Cone argued that more than thirty years after the beginning of black theology we are still waiting for Euro-Americans to engage us in serious dialogue. Cone's point is not that Euro-Americans must accept or become black theologians, but that there should be a willingness on their part to engage in serious dialogue on the task of theology in the American context.

The suspicion works both ways and is not mutually exclusive. Some Euro-American Wesleyan theologians, arguing they are staying true to Wesley, are suspicious of the way in which some African American theologians privilege the black experience. Some Wesleyans think that by focusing on the black experience African American theology loses its objectivity and ceases to move toward a holistic theological perspective. To put it politely, the black experience may be valid for African

Americans, but it is not a valid lens for illuminating a holistic understanding of God.

The question is, *Can the particularity of the black experience illuminate holistic ideas about God?* Experience can test certain understandings of Scripture, and in some instances even take on a more pronounced role when Scripture is silent, but experience is never the starting point for one's theological construction. Some Wesleyan theologians in staying true to Wesley privilege Scripture over experience. They are suspicious of some African American theologians because they advocate for a dialectic between Scripture and experience. Ultimately this suspicion by some Wesleyan theologians calls into question the practices of African American theologians seeking justice because they have focused on the particularity of the black experience while ignoring the oppression suffered by Euro-Americans.

This hermeneutic of suspicion by both sides is destructive because it perpetuates an ideal of just-us. Both African American and Euro-American theologians become concerned with just their issues, forgetting the common Christian goal of true justice. The hermeneutic of suspicion reinforces preconceived notions about the other, and both sides stay on their side of the fence. Interestingly, some individuals (usually within the UMC) want to knock the fence down immediately without addressing the just-us issues between these communities.

Therefore a recurring theme within Methodism is the issue of some form of a merger among the Pan-Methodist denominations. Before moving too quickly in developing merger strategies for all of the Pan-Methodist denominations, we should remember the history of the Central Jurisdiction's incorporation into The United Methodist Church. The Central Jurisdiction was created in 1939 as the only racial jurisdiction within the then Methodist Episcopal Church.

James Thomas comments:

> During the negotiations leading to union, several proposals were set forth, but all of the major ones recommended either a separate racial structure or an all–African American Methodist Church which the then-members of the church would be asked to join voluntarily. Just as slavery had been the determining factor in Methodist relations with African Americans, so also segregation had determined these relations during discussions on union.[5]

The Central Jurisdiction began merging into The United Methodist Church in 1968, and the process lasted for five years.[6] The merging of the Central Jurisdiction into The United Methodist Church addressed the racial issue of preserving a separate jurisdiction only for African Americans. The merger did not address the issue of two existing churches within one denomination. In essence, The United Methodist Church has white congregations and black congregations (today it has Latino, Korean, Native American, and so forth). The merger ended the explicit racism created by the Central Jurisdiction, but it did not end the separation of the races.

Moving toward a Pan-Methodist theology does not necessitate forcing integration. It does, however, mean raising the question, *What is the purpose of merging?* If merging means we continue to live out just-us under the rubric of one umbrella, then what difference has merging meant for all parties involved? The idea of merging at times seems beneficial, but in practice is more of a romantic hope for something new that seems promising. For instance, an AME pastor in Kansas City commented that the UMC pastor in his town continually talked about the need for merging.[7] When the AME pastor invited the pastor and his church to his congregation (the UMC pastor was the guest preacher), only the UMC pastor and his spouse actually showed up. I do not think this is an uncommon story and it points to the difficulty of changing actual practices. Both sides are entrenched in their just-us perspectives, resulting in little or no dialogue.

These problems within Methodism have resulted in theological and practical just-us. I am not suggesting this one book will resolve these problems, but it is important to explore certain theological themes that may help engender new dialogues within Methodism today. Three theological themes that will be further developed in the following chapters are: (1) identity, (2) methodology, and (3) reconciliation. The theme of identity raises issues around the meaning of a Christian identity versus a black identity or a Wesleyan identity. Can these different identities intersect with one another? Methodological issues focus on questions pertaining to the use of experience and how to create intersections between African American theology and Wesleyan theology. The issue of reconciliation helps us think about what this term means in an attempt to move toward a Pan-Methodist soteriology. Thinking about reconciliation also means asking hard teleological questions that influence how we understand justice.

Justice

Having outlined some of the challenges in moving toward a Pan-Methodist theology, let me briefly foreshadow some of the benefits. All Methodist denominations at some level agree that justice is an important issue. The method of achieving justice often differs by denomination and, truthfully, by individual churches within each denomination. For example, the AMEZ denomination has a strong legacy of great African American leaders like Frederick Douglass and Sojourner Truth, who worked for structural changes in society. The AME denomination has been successful in working for urban renewal in different places in the country (the Reverend Floyd Flake in New York is just one example). The UMC has its social creed, which states many of its beliefs concerning justice issues and appropriate practices.

Thinking about justice from a Pan-Methodist perspective requires drawing on the richness from the various Methodist denominations. I will highlight three possible insights that moving toward a Pan-Methodist theology offers in thinking about justice issues. First, rethinking the theme of identity from a Pan-Methodist perspective offers new possibilities for loving God and loving one's neighbor. The focus on identity is an issue that separates African American and Wesleyan theological perspectives, and when this separation becomes structural (that is, separate African American Methodist denominations), practicing loving one's neighbor is often defined differently.

In moving toward a Pan-Methodist theological perspective difficult questions must be answered concerning what love of God and love of neighbor look like in practice. Almost all Christians agree loving God and loving their neighbor is an important New Testament theme, but not all Christians contextualize the practice of love in response to their neighbor. Moving toward a Pan-Methodist theology will not magically change how love of God and neighbor are practiced. I do believe moving toward a Pan-Methodist theology can open up possibilities for practicing love of God and neighbor that integrates useful insights from African American and Wesleyan theologies.

Second, I believe rethinking methodological issues between African American and Wesleyan theologies must focus on the role of experience. If justice and not just-us is the ultimate goal, then thinking about experience differently is important. One possible intersection for African American and Wesleyan theologies is grounding experience in soteriology, an approach that allows both perspectives to preserve fundamental claims.

Practically, moving to a soteriological focus enables African American theology to preserve its emphasis on liberation and Wesleyan theology to preserve its emphasis on the *ordo salutis*. A focus on soteriology opens up possibilities for how love and justice can be related concretely without negating the emphasis of African American or Wesleyan theologies. Many African American theologians perceive love and justice as practices lived out on this side of salvation, and many Wesleyan theologians would agree that these practices begin in the here and now. The intersection of these perspectives can offer new insights into the role individuals and communities can play in the justice process. Methodological issues would no longer have to be a stumbling block in working on justice concerns.

Third, rethinking reconciliation from a Pan-Methodist perspective means an analysis of power structures. Reconciliation should not be a form of cheap grace that just places different communities under one umbrella. Determining the purpose of the reconciliation and the power structures involved in the reconciling process must be a part of the conversation. This does not mean that if power differentials exist there is no way to move forward; it means proposing a different way to move forward.

Moving toward a Pan-Methodist perspective can best be seen as a kind of engaging friendship. An engaging friendship is one that allows the other space while maintaining a sustained relationship with the other. The hope is to move to a deeper relationship by reconceptualizing the power differentials that exist. Practically, this approach creates space in which partnerships can be formed to work on justice-related issues, but it does not necessarily dictate the ongoing form the relationship must take.

In advocating movement toward a Pan-Methodist theology I am not proposing that African American and Wesleyan theological perspectives are inadequate. Contrarily, I am proposing that new insights are possible that can open up new possibilities for shifting the focus from just-us to justice. It is time such a dialogue takes place as we struggle in Methodism with continuing diversity. I hope other voices will join the dialogue because I represent just one perspective in thinking about a different theological vision.

CHAPTER 1

HISTORICAL ROOTS OF JUST-US

Black and white Methodists found themselves on opposite sides of debates concerning social and political issues, theological doctrines, and even styles of worship from the very beginnings of Methodism in the United States. In the 1760s, laypersons, including some black men and women, started the first American Methodist Societies. "Negro men and women were accepted into [early American] Methodism with whites, irrespective of their race or slave status."[1] For various theological and economic reasons the Methodist Episcopal Church shifted its position and eventually split over the issue of slavery. Frederick Norwood points out that even Francis Asbury, who picked up John Wesley's antislavery gauntlet in the United States, compromises on the issue of slavery.[2] Asbury and some other Euro-American Methodists sought to keep the church together (North and South) even if this meant supporting slavery, with which they disagreed in principle.

The tension slavery caused, experienced by Asbury and others, was not uncommon during the beginnings of Methodism. In a cursory look at history, two major themes emerge confronting African American and Euro-American Methodists: (1) because of slavery American Methodism has had to broaden its theological base; (2) the historical roots of just-us run deep in American culture and this is reflected in American Methodism. The theological lens holding the two themes together is my claim that Euro-American and African American Methodists developed divergent views of the doctrine of salvation—views that translated into different theological agendas.

Slavery

Othal Lakey, in his comprehensive history of the CME Church, discusses the impact slavery had on American religion and specifically on Methodism. He writes:

> We here maintain that the organization and history of the CME Church is reflective of the fact that American slavery—that peculiar institution—constituted the formative experience for the existence of Black Americans. By this we mean that the history of Black people, and especially the nature of Black religion, must be understood in light of slavery as the milieu in which the personal, social, and spiritual life of Black Americans was shaped; the condition out of which they emerged as a race; and the legacy of which has impinged upon every aspect of their lives.[3]

Lakey captures how ensnarling slavery was for African Americans. No part of life was untouched by the institution of slavery, and its legacy continues to haunt African Americans today. Lakey recognizes that part of the legacy that must be told is how slavery influenced the way blacks were incorporated into organized church life.

For American Methodism, a vital part of this legacy includes why Africans were attracted to Methodist classes and not to other denominations. Lakey suggests it was the "spiritual fervor, preaching style, structure of the societies, [and] doctrinal simplicity" that made Methodism attractive to Africans.[4] In fact, in 1828 one out of every four Methodists was African.[5] During the establishment of Methodism, African Americans were an integral part of the story because the message of salvation was meant for both blacks and whites.[6]

The message was more experiential than that of other denominations and allowed slaves to participate.[7] The reason Africans resonated with the experiential message was that it reminded them of their own African religious traditions.[8] The key point is that early Methodists were able to connect with African slaves, who became a significant numerical presence in the movement. Lakey credits a sincere emphasis on salvation as one of the factors for the growth of Methodism among slaves.[9]

Lakey also suggests that even at this early stage just-us soteriological concerns started taking root. He outlines three reasons some slave owners wanted to evangelize their slaves. First, evangelizing slaves was perceived as a way of countering antislavery sentiment.[10] Slave owners needed to justify owning and treating humans in a deplorable manner. The slave owners' message of salvation was that the souls of slaves could be saved while their bodies stayed enslaved.[11] A separation between the body and soul in terms of salvation was created to justify dehumanizing the body. The separation of the body and soul was given Episcopal legitimacy when Asbury compromised his staunch antislavery stance, buying into justifications for the institution.[12]

Second, evangelism to slaves was perceived as a "spiritual tonic."[13] The goal here was to make slaves more docile. Many slave owners became convinced that their slaves would become better servants if they heard certain scriptural references. This, of course, meant that preachers were very particular about what they preached to the slaves, and messages on obedience were a high priority. It also meant keeping slaves from reading so that they could not read the Bible themselves and learn what the Euro-American preachers were omitting.

Third, some Euro-American preachers and missionaries were able to feel good about themselves by helping the poor slaves. The thinking behind this was that Africans were just heathens and white preachers were doing them a service by bringing them the gospel. The thought was, "We are civilizing the savages." This approach reinforced the superiority of those bringing the gospel over those needing the gospel. Moreover, it created a way to deal with guilt for some of the Euro-American preachers and missionaries who felt like they were "giving back" to society.[14]

Along these same lines was the attempt by some Southerners to distinguish between personal sins and social evils.[15] The focus was on personal sins and not on social evils. The state-run institution of slavery was a social evil, but the business of the church was personal sin.[16] The idea was to help those benefiting from the institution of slavery to feel better about themselves, protect their property rights, and separate their personal actions from a social structure over which they had limited control. The separation of personal sins from social evil enabled many Euro-American Methodists to benefit from slave labor without having to feel guilty.

Northern Complicity

Even today, the tendency is for the South to be denigrated because it supported slavery, and for the North to be exalted. The truth is not that easy. The fact that an African American lived in the North and was technically free did not necessarily translate into neighborly treatment by Euro-Americans. Three out of the four black Methodist denominations started in free states (AME, AMEZ, and African Union Church).

Richard Allen gives us insight into how African Americans were generally treated by some Northern Methodist congregations. He writes:

> A number of us usually attended St. George's church in Fourth street; and when the colored people began to get numerous in attending the church, they moved us from the seats we usually sat on, and placed us around the wall, and on Sabbath morning we went to church and the sexton stood at the door, and told us to go in the gallery. He told us to go, and we would see where to sit. We expected to take the seats over the ones we formerly occupied below, not knowing any better.[17]

Explicit in Allen's comments is the fact that African Americans were being ushered into new seats that were not comparable to the ones in which they previously sat. Implicit in his comments is the fact that African Americans were assigned certain seats even before the infamous incident at Saint George's. Although Allen and the other African Americans were free, they were not treated the same as Euro-American members of the congregation.

Certainly not every congregation in the North treated African Americans unjustly, but the separation of the races after 1800 became common practice.[18] It seems unlikely that the African Americans left the classes and societies just for the sake of starting something new. Explicitly stated by Allen, and reading between the lines of other similar situations, it is not a far stretch to suggest many African Americans left because they were not being treated as full partners.

Even the blacks that stayed in the Methodist Episcopal Church started to worship separately from Euro-Americans. In 1867 two of the Northern conferences had churches with entirely black clergy and laity; most of the others were predominantly white.[19] William Gravely suggests the segregation of the races in the North was because of the "inability of the churches to transcend racial distinctions in their own membership."[20] Although many Northern cities did not enslave African Americans, it is a reach to say they were treated the same as whites.

If the South focused on separating the body and the soul, then the North focused on a complete separation of the races. Although African Americans were free in the North, this did not translate into nonracial ecclesial practices. William Gravely writes: "The class meeting structure was, therefore, the earliest separate African Methodist group experience. As racial separatism increased and the number of African converts grew, the class gave way to the racially distinct congregation or society."[21] In the South the idea was that the salvation of the soul did not mean the freedom of the body. In the North the question of salvation was not explicit in the separation of the races, but it did imply the races were expected to work out their salvation separately. The long-term impact of this separation was different soteriological emphases between blacks and whites even though the ultimate goal of "heaven" remains common language.

Some Euro-Americans reinforced the separation of the races in the North by treating African Americans as second-class individuals (they were less than citizens). Richard Allen reports in his memoirs:

> Rev. Bishop Asbury sent for me to meet him at Henry Gaff's. I did so. He told me he wished me to travel with him. He told me in the slave countries, Carolina and other places, I must not intermix with the slaves, and I would frequently have to sleep in his carriage, and he would allow me my victuals and clothes. I told him I would not travel with him on these conditions. He asked me my reason. I told him if I was taken sick, who was to support me? And that I thought people ought to lay up something while they were able, to support themselves in time of sickness or old age. He said that was as much as he got, his victuals and clothes. I told him he would be taken care of, let his afflictions be as they were, or let him be taken sick where he would, he would be taken care of; but I doubted whether it would be the case with myself.[22]

The dialogue between Allen and Asbury is quite telling related to the treatment of African Americans. Allen perceptibly understands that Asbury's argument is faulty because of the difference between how blacks and whites were treated. Asbury as a European male and bishop benefited from the structure of society in a way that Allen could not. African Americans were a part of the church in the North numerically but had no real voice in its governance or theology.

Asbury does eventually ordain Allen as a local deacon in 1799, but even this ordination comes with second-class ramifications because Allen was not connected to the conference.[23] Those connected to the Methodist Church in the North treated not only Allen in this manner but other blacks as well.[24] The undeniable consequence was that Northern Euro-American Methodists were the only ones who governed the church and determined its theological moorings. African Americans could support the efforts of Euro-Americans, but "true" salvation was only possible within a white ecclesial structure. The Methodist Episcopal Church's noninclusion of African American voices in key ecclesial positions supports this strong statement. The idea inherent in this Northern complicity suggests that separating personal and social salvation was just as easily accomplished in the North as it was in the South, thus negating a more holistic view of theology.

Just-us in Methodism and American Culture

The backdrop for the way many Southern and Northern Methodists perceived African Americans helps one understand how these ideas developed into just-us mind-sets. Four attitudes that were prevalent in many Euro-Americans in both the North and South during the eighteenth and nineteenth centuries are: the idea of innate superiority, social incompatibility with blacks, a narrowing morality, and Christian paternalism. For instance, the idea of separating personal sin from social sin gets translated into a method for narrowing one's moral focus to redefine soteriology in a direction that often negates social ills. Certainly it is an oversimplification to create exact matches between all four mind-sets listed above with a corresponding issue related to Northern or Southern Methodists. It is not an oversimplification to argue that the attitudes of just-us I will describe are, at least in part, rooted in issues related to social, political, and moral issues.

Innate Superiority

Many white Americans believed themselves naturally superior to African Americans. They had to. Sociologists often describe the mechanisms of oppression in terms of seeing the oppressed as "the other." It was not possible to enslave Africans if one thought of them as human beings like oneself.

James McPherson writes:

> One of the most formidable obstacles to the abolition of slavery and the extension of equal rights to free Negroes was the widespread popular and scientific belief, North as well as South, in the innate inferiority of

was climbing a mountain to change social attitudes in the United States. He foreshadows what a social caste system ultimately meant for American society and Christians in particular:

> But equality at the polls is not the only work laid upon the coming government. There must be such a disposition of its patronage, such a steadfast expression of its conviction, such an employment of its influence, as will tend to the abolition of the whole mass of prejudice that still defiles the national heart. I am aware that this evil cannot be utterly abolished by any enactments. The leprosy lies deep within. It dwells in our churches, in our souls, in our education, in society.... It still leads us to erect barriers between us and our kindred, and to make us and them talk of "our race" as if they and we had a different parentage, Savior, and eternity.[44]

Haven's insight into the just-us many Euro-Americans in society promote again suggests different soteriological interests between African Americans and Euro-Americans. Is it possible as a Christian to practice segregation but also to argue for the same understanding of salvation?

Another form of social segregation in American society generally and among Methodists in particular was social class awareness. Social class awareness had racial implications, but was not strictly a racial issue. This newfound social awareness was a result of economic, political, and educational gains made by many within the Methodist church.[45] I believe what was occurring in Methodism was a reflection of American society during that time.[46] Certain elements within Methodism and society as a whole started distinguishing themselves socially from the more enthusiastic (high-spirited) expressions of the denomination.

This separation from the more extemporaneous expressions of the faith meant an erosion of the old camp meetings, class meetings, and love feasts.[47] The attraction of the camp meeting, class meeting, and love feast for African Americans had always been that they could openly express themselves. Methodists and Baptists were successful in attracting African Americans because their message was much more experiential and allowed blacks to participate.[48] As more Euro-American Methodists became socially mobile, they sought to distance themselves from those who emphasized these characteristics of the denomination. The attitude of many Methodists created another form of just-us that affected not only African Americans but also other poor immigrants not considered a part of the emerging upwardly mobile social class movement. Upward social mobility was more highly valued than churches reflecting a vision of God's kingdom.

Narrowing Morality

Along with a shift in social awareness came a shift that narrowed the focus of holiness. Wesley taught and preached personal and social holiness. Wesley once commented, "There is no holiness but social holiness."[49] It is unfair to read Wesley's understanding of social holiness as social activism in the manner that we use the term today. It is more accurate to interpret Wesley's understanding of social holiness as the love of God shed abroad in every heart in the community. Wesley's understanding of social holiness does not exclude social activism aimed at mirroring the mercy, love, and justice of Jesus the Christ. Certainly Wesley believed his perspective of holiness was inconsistent with enslaving others or with the blatant racism found in many Northern churches. Ultimately Wesley sought an organic understanding of holiness that includes both inward and outward transformation.

Within the American context, this understanding of holiness was redefined and personal holiness became privileged. Many Euro-American Methodists failed to maintain Wesley's understanding of holiness. Personal and social holiness were often viewed separately or reinterpreted as a two-step process. The Christian life was developed along the lines of personal holiness, and responsibility to the life of the community was viewed through the lens of personal holiness and not as a means of transforming society. For example, arguing that the institution of slavery was a societal issue and not a sin emphasized personal holiness because it enabled slave-holding Southern Methodists to argue that they were still acting morally.

A figure who was instrumental in moving Methodism (especially in the North) toward a two-step understanding of holiness was Phoebe Palmer. Although it was not her intent to develop what I am calling a two-step process of holiness, Palmer tended not to mix her theology, moral writings, or speeches with her social commitments. Palmer was against slavery and active in the temperance movement during her life.[50] She was socially aware and her understanding of holiness supported her stances on slavery and temperance; but in her Tuesday meetings she developed a pattern that emphasized "earnest prayer, study of scripture, spontaneous testimony to the fully cleansing activity of the spirit, radical personal openness, and frank encounter concerning the need for present holiness."[51] This same pattern was followed in many African American prayer services or class meetings during this same time.[52] It is unfair to say only Euro-Americans emphasized personal holiness.

The difference is some African Americans directly challenged social evil in their theological and moral speeches (writings). Maria Stewart, who was connected to the AME Church in Boston, was also the first woman to lecture publicly in the United States and leave manuscripts for us to read.[53] Although Stewart's writings are not as extensive as Palmer's, she embodied much of what Palmer advocated concerning personal holiness while challenging social evil. In a farewell speech made at the African Meeting House in Boston in 1833, Stewart challenged other African Americans to be better morally and assured them that God sees their persecution at the hand of Euro-Americans. For instance, concerning social evil Stewart argued, "But a God of infinite purity will not regard the prayers of those who hold religion in one hand, and prejudice, sin and pollution in the other; he will not regard the prayers of self-righteousness and hypocrisy."[54]

Stewart and other African Americans were able to keep an appropriate tension between personal holiness and social holiness. They challenged the Christian community, and especially the Euro-American Christian community, to be transformed in a way that demonstrated the love of God shed abroad in their lives. Palmer lived out a transformed life, but one could—and I believe many did—separate her communal commitments from her insights into holiness. As personal holiness was privileged, it became the lens through which social holiness was viewed and even the doctrine of salvation was interpreted.

Just-us in this instance was subtle because both blacks and whites promoted personal holiness. The difference was many Euro-Americans privileged personal holiness at the cost of devaluing social holiness while many African Americans sought to maintain a healthy tension between personal and social holiness. Sadly, today in many African American church communities this healthy tension has disappeared, reflecting how pervasive the roots of just-us run.

Christian Paternalism

Even before the Civil War, many Euro-Americans in the North and the South believed some sort of solution needed to be initiated to resolve the status of free African Americans. Slaveholders in the South were worried that free African Americans would try to aid those still in bondage, disrupting their work force. In the North many Euro-Americans felt African Americans were in such a limbo status that a more permanent solution was needed. The solution offered by many was the formation of the American Society for Colonizing the Free People of Color of the United States in 1816. The organization was a popular solution because it seemed like a compromise that both Southerners and Northerners could endorse. Donald Mathews writes:

> More a state of mind than a plan of action, the colonization cause enticed men to placate their consciences, conciliate the slaveholders, and shed tears over the plight of the Negroes whom they hoped to ship to Africa. Initially recommended to the Church as a part of the rising interests in missions, the movement embraced enough moral sentiment against slavery to appeal to the Methodist antislavery inheritance.[55]

The plan for colonization was not only supported by Methodists but by many corners in American society.

The plan itself was a political solution that would enable free African Americans to reestablish themselves on the coast of Africa. Liberia became the proposed site of settlement, with the hope that free African Americans would willingly return to their homeland. From the perspective of many Euro-Americans who supported the colonization effort, it was not a politically based solution, but rather a missionary effort to aid free African Americans.[56]

Stewart points out that those in favor of colonization are blind to their own interests, which are not necessarily the interests of most African Americans. She goes on to recommend that if those supporting the colonizationists' project really are friends of Africans, then they should put their money into schools for educating blacks and not sink it into overseas projects.[57] Stewart's point is that Euro-Americans should have talked with African Americans to learn their interest and not try to make that determination without their input.

Walker, like Stewart, also believed the colonization project was a selfish maneuver by some Euro-Americans. He saw the real issues as preventing race mixing and getting rid of a perceived hindrance.[58] Nathan Bangs, in his fight against William Garrison, who opposed the colonization plan, suggested that those thinking like Garrison were really for race mixing.[59] Bangs's comments about race mixing were meant to be derogatory and further proof for why the colonization plan was necessary.

Bangs and others who supported the colonization plan were simply trying to answer (albeit for themselves) what should be done with free African Americans. Free African Americans were not slaves, so they could not be forced into labor, but they were not equal to exercise their rights in society. The problem this created in the North for many Euro-Americans was what to do with a group of people who were segregated from the benefits of white society. In reality, many Euro-Americans did not want to associate with blacks and perceived African Americans as a nuisance. The Euro-Americans who supported the colonization plan were not acting on a missionary impulse out of concern for free African Americans; they were more concerned with resolving the problem free African Americans presented.

Many Euro-Americans did not perceive the colonization effort as a political issue because it was a compromise that benefited them. They merely couched it in the language of a missionary effort to aid free Africans. African Americans perceived it as political and paternalistic because it affected their future. This divide created a form of just-us between blacks and whites around whose self-interest is being served when dealing with controversial, racially based issues. African Americans were, and continue to be, suspicious of Euro-American benevolence because they believe, based on previous experience, that there might be a hidden agenda. Many Euro-Americans believe they are helping African Americans, but do so without sufficient input.

It is tough to be "saved" together when just-us concerns maintain a divide between the races. Why would some African Americans want to work out their salvation with Euro-Americans who are self-serving? What would working toward a common interest really look like for blacks and whites? These are tough questions that will be addressed throughout this book. A real issue is, *Are we living as though there are two paths to salvation that never intersect?*

CHAPTER 2

EXPERIENCING JUST-US

We cannot get far in developing a Pan-Methodist theology without addressing methodology. This is a difficult issue because African American and Wesleyan theologians typically have different understandings of the nature of experience and the role it plays in theology. Experience is essential to both, and is one of the four sources of what Albert Outler coined the "Wesleyan Quadrilateral." Although the usefulness of the Quadrilateral has been increasingly questioned, many Wesleyan scholars, following Wesley, still privilege the way Scripture informs and shapes Christian experience. Many African American scholars, however, perceive an interdependent relationship between the biblical text and experience. These scholars suggest that it is impossible to separate one's experiences from how a text is interpreted.

A Pan-Methodist theology will need to do more than simply assert that both Wesleyan and African American theologies contribute to a multifaceted understanding of experience (which they do). To be genuinely Pan-Methodist, such a theology must also show the interrelation of these views of experience. It should not only draw on the respective strengths of both approaches but also offer an approach of its own that is more theologically adequate than either of them alone.

Wesleyan Methodology

Although there are various Wesleyan methodological approaches and understandings of how experience is used as a source for theological reflection, most Wesleyan scholars share two assumptions: (1) that John and Charles Wesley's sermons, hymns, and other writings should play a guiding role in Wesleyan theology, and (2) that John Wesley's focus on the *via salutis* has to be central to any Wesleyan theology. It is these assumptions that ground their understanding of the role of experience in Wesleyan theology.

In a theological sense, the term *experience* can be interpreted in various ways. Randy L. Maddox offers a humorous example that speaks to the ambiguity of this term:

> A patient of a group medical practice is slated for surgery and insists on "the benefit of experience" in the operation. A puzzled nurse responds, "Well, if you insist, but most of our patients consider it a benefit to have anesthesia so that they do not experience the operation!" The patient retorts rather curtly, "I did not mean that I want to feel the operation, but that I want a physician with experience in this procedure." "In that case," the helpful nurse replies, "you will want Dr. White. She has not performed the surgery before, but she has had it herself, so she will understand what you are going through!"[1]

There is then a real challenge in comprehending what "experience" means. Is experience the ability to feel something or to be aware of it subjectively?[2] Is experience being able to relate to something someone else has gone through?[3] Maddox discusses six different understandings of experience common to Wesley, as well as later ideas of experience as mediated. He does not, however, explore the cultural connotations of experience or how the shared traumatic experiences of groups like African Americans shape their perception of life. Wesley's understanding and use of experience does not privilege the cultural perspectives that are important to many African Americans.

Wesley limits the way he uses experience because he fears that some interpretations of the term can promote misinformed readings of the Bible. In his sermon, "The Witness of the Spirit II," Wesley argues, "Experience is not sufficient to prove a doctrine which is not founded on scripture. . . . Therefore experience is properly alleged to confirm it."[4] Experience played an important role in ministry for Wesley, because it gave him a means to analyze the lived experiences of individuals to determine if they were actually practicing what Scripture outlined. Many Wesleyan scholars agree with Wesley that experience should not become a governing lens for interpreting the Bible and more properly should be used to analyze the way we live out Scripture. The way of salvation in Wesleyan theology is not driven by one's subjective interpretation of the text, but by the way the text shapes the person. Maddox clarifies how Wesley uses experience to test whether Scripture is properly informing us:

> Wesley's appeal to experience in doctrinal decisions was typically to an external, long-term, communal reality: his observation of his life, the lives of his Methodist people, and human life in general. Consideration of such experience served primarily to test understandings of Scripture. It took a more conscious constructive role only where he believed that Scripture was silent or inconclusive on an issue. Throughout, its subordination to Scripture was clear. Such a use of experience stands up well to modern methodological insights.[5]

Many Wesleyan scholars agree with Maddox that reclaiming a Wesleyan methodology can be helpful for theological reflection today.

The challenge, however, for many Wesleyan theologians in the United States is how to determine the limiting and limited role experience should play in theological reflection. Reclaiming a Wesleyan understanding of experience can be helpful, but it categorically limits the way experience must be understood within Pan-Methodism. The fact that African American theology begins with the experiences of black men and women therefore is problematic for some Wesleyans because, by their very definition of theology, the shared experience of a group is not a sufficient starting point for theological reflection. If one begins theological reflection with experience, then, using Wesley's logic, the individual runs the risk of idolatry. The person's focus is on the community rather than on Christ. This means that a person runs the risk of growing into the community image rather than into the image of Christ as described by the Bible. Such Wesleyans would argue that becoming more Christlike requires conforming to the biblical text and not bringing preconceived ideas about how the text should conform to one's own or one's community's experiences and practices.

By using this approach, Wesleyan scholars seek to avoid experience simply becoming one's subjective interpretation of the Bible. Experience can confirm the truth of Scripture by the living testimony of Christians, but experience is not qualified to inform Scripture in a manner that invalidates the whole tenor of the Bible. The challenge to African American scholars is whether their use of experience (mis)informs their understanding of the Scripture in a particular manner that prejudices the whole tenor of the Bible. If the answer is yes, then they need to rethink their use of experience. Certainly for those within the Methodist tradition, the argument is that Wesley provides an alternative way to think about the use of experience in theological reflection.

Wesleyan scholars, such as Theodore Runyon, argue experience is not just an episode of felt intensity (for example, Wesley's Aldersgate experience) but of truly developing a pattern of experiences that form one's disposition (affections).[6] We will know that we are developing this pattern of right experiences when we are known by our fruits—love, joy, and peace.[7] The right experience is not about what makes one happy as an individual but rather is about actively becoming more like Christ.

Runyon uses the term *orthopathy* to talk about the right experience.[8] For Runyon, experience is properly understood in concrete rather than abstract terms. "Only as we are incorporated into God's renewing activity are we able to speak with the authority born out of the experience of God as *our* Creator," he writes.[9] Runyon's point is that not everything qualifies as the right Christian experience, and for those following Wesley, it manifests itself in the way we are incorporated into God's saving work in this world. Runyon is advocating for an understanding of Christian experience that is not neutral, and resists being controlled by personal and communal particularities. I am not clear on why advocating is before restricting.

Scott Jones describes the tension Wesleyans negotiate between Scripture and experience by stating: "Because Scripture is understood as guiding the individual to salvation, which can be experienced, those experiences which confirm Scripture's teaching also serve as the goal for the Christian life."[10] As Jones points out, Wesleyan scholars attempt to maintain Wesley's emphasis on the whole tenor of the Bible moving us toward salvation, and our Christian experiences can help us affirm this goal.

The strength of a Wesleyan approach for theological reflection on experience is the idea that a right experience exists. A Wesleyan understanding of the right experience that suggests holding someone made in the image of God as a slave is inconsistent with God's plan of salvation for the earth. An inference we can draw from a Wesleyan understanding of experience is that faith claims have no meaning if one's practices are not congruent with those claims. For Wesleyans, there is an implicit tension between faith claims and practices: the practices validate the faith claims; faith claims validate the importance of proper practices. Wesleyans, however, are clear that by "practices" they mean that one's disposition has been properly formed by the whole tenor of the Bible. An important aspect of the whole tenor of the Bible is that a right experience exists that all Christians are called to emulate—movement toward Christ likeness. For Wesleyans, it is not possible to claim love of God and love of neighbor while enslaving other humans. Thus, experience testifies to the reality of Christian faith claims by allowing humanity to observe in practical ways if Christians are, in fact, acting justly toward God and their neighbor.

African American Methodology

African American scholars do not negate a Wesleyan perspective of experience, but they do take a somewhat different route with respect to experience. One of the major reasons for this is that their assumptions differ from those of most Wesleyan scholars in the following ways: (1) many African American scholars utilize black sources as a starting point for their work, and (2) most African American scholars believe the idea of liberation is central to their theological perspective. African American scholars believe that beginning with the black experience makes it possible to find the resources necessary to overcome structural oppression and eventually to move toward true liberation and justice. Therefore, slavery is often the starting point for many black scholars since it is the one major shared experience of African Americans in the United States. The impact of slavery on African Americans cannot be emphasized enough, and this is especially true in relation to religion. Slaves encountered Christianity through the lens of European preachers and missionaries, who had certain prejudices in what they taught. Kelly Brown Douglas claims this is one of the reasons the story of Ham serving his brothers was so important to the institution of slavery.[11] The slave owners needed to reinforce in the African slaves that their destiny was to serve whites.

African American scholars, recognizing the impact of slavery, begin with the assumption that experience in a theological sense is not a neutral idea because European Christians have compromised it. James Cone describes how one of his encounters with a Euro-American colleague helped him understand how compromised the language of experience is in theological circles. He writes, concerning the colleague, "He is saying... 'unless you black people learn to think like us white folks, using our rules, then we will not listen to you.'"[12] The point is that there is an acceptable way, utilizing the methodology of Western European theologians, for engaging in theology, and specifically for understanding the term *experience*. Experience, say such theologians, should be understood from the perspective of Western European thought and not from the perspective of African Americans. To assume the word *experience* is just a neutral theological term that has the same meaning for everyone is incompatible not only with some Wesleyan theological thinking but with the experiences of many African American Methodists in America.

Many African American scholars differ from many Wesleyan theologians concerning the use of experience because of their focus on the context in which theology occurs. Cone argues it is impossible to separate his experiences as an African American living in Bearden, Arkansas, from his theological reflection. He avows, "I am a *black* theologian! I therefore must approach the subject of theology in light of the black Church and what it means in a society dominated by white people."[13] Cone's point is that trying to do theology as an African American without taking seriously one's lived reality ignores the factors shaping one's theological perspective. For instance, African Americans within the Methodist tradition who disregard the impact of slavery and racism on their theological perspective are not seriously engaging the factors that formed their denominational experiences.

How do many African American scholars make use of the term *experience?* If Wesleyans argue that the whole tenor of the Bible should shape our experiences, then many African American scholars begin with the particularity of the black experience and relate it to the Bible. It is important to note that for many African American scholars the Bible is still the primary source of theological reflection, but experience is in tension with the Bible. The Bible is read through the particularity of African American experiences as a means for interpreting meaning in the lives of black people.

African American scholars begin with the particular because they do not believe it is possible for a neutral Christian experience to supersede their own particular experiences. In the case of African Americans who have experienced oppression, this means that liberation from oppressive structures becomes a hermeneutical approach to the text.[14] Unlike Wesleyans, African American scholars do not believe the Bible stands above experience, but that one's experiences also inform how the Bible is approached. An example can illuminate the different starting points. Wesleyan scholars who begin with love of God and move to love of neighbor perceive loving God as informing one's love for the neighbor. An African American biblical emphasis nuances the Wesleyan approach by arguing, "If you have not loved your brother or sister whom you have seen, then how can you love God whom you have not seen?"[15] Because many African American scholars emphasize liberation, they shift the starting point to love of those being oppressed (the black community) as the appropriate way to loving God.

Cone helps clarify the relationship between the Bible and black experiences by noting that black experiences are not the "truth" and that Jesus the Christ revealed in the Scriptures is the Truth.[16] A normative connection, for many African American scholars, is the motif of liberation and the fact that Jesus has experienced the plight of the oppressed, meaning that Jesus also stands in judgment of the oppressed. Jesus stands in judgment of the oppressed as God because he takes on suffering. The oppressed are "privileged," but this does not relieve them of obedience to the commandment of loving God and neighbor to which all humans are called.

Cone's point is that black experiences must still be judged by the gospel and particularly the "Truth" of Jesus the Christ. The particularity of the black experience must always be in relationship to the whole tenor of the Bible.

The reason African American scholars understand experience in this way is they are trying to make sense out of the actual lived experiences of African Americans in a Christian context. Cone makes the point, "A theology created for comfortable white suburbia could not answer questions that blacks were asking in their struggle for dignity in the wretched conditions of the riot-torn ghettos of U.S. cities."[17] Cone is suggesting that it is only by beginning with the black experience and putting the particularity of the black experience into conversation with the biblical message that African Americans can begin to overcome oppressive structures. It is a tenuous balance that African American scholars seek to maintain, but it is one that is important for their liberation motif.

The strength of an African American perspective on experience is the opposite of its weakness. An African American perspective is grounded in the particularity of the black experience, meaning it is not abstract and instead focuses on the lived reality of a community. By focusing on the particularity of the black experience, it clarifies the way in which the motif of liberation informs how the Bible is interpreted, and how the Bible informs the motif of liberation. Jacquelyn Grant describes the important tension that liberation theologians seek to maintain when treating black experience as a "starting point but not a stopping point."[18] Grant's point is critical because it refutes the claim that beginning with black experiences becomes the end to which all African American theology moves. In actuality, African American scholars use black experiences to develop the right theological questions for the community before moving to how these questions relate to larger doctrinal issues.

Moving toward a Pan-Methodist Methodology

African American and Wesleyan scholars have different understandings of experience, and hence different methodologies when it comes to the theological task. A Pan-Methodist theology must take into consideration these differences and try to find some common ground that maintains the integrity of both positions. Two assumptions that are helpful in achieving this goal are: (1) the importance of honoring the Methodist tradition,[19] and (2) moving toward a shared epistemology that values soteriology. I think both of these assumptions maintain the integrity of African American and Wesleyan scholars and move us toward a Pan-Methodist methodology.

Moving toward a Pan-Methodist methodology means experience has to be understood not only in the ways outlined by some Wesleyans in part one of this chapter but must also include the shared cultural experiences of African Americans. Ignoring the shared cultural experiences of African Americans helps perpetuate the idea that Methodist theology must be centered on Eurocentric experiences. Let me be clear that it is not only African Americans whose cultural experiences have been ignored by the majority group, this methodology is applicable to other oppressed groups as well. Including the shared cultural experiences of African Americans (and other oppressed groups) opens up Methodist theology to move in a different direction, encompassing Euro-American and African American understandings of experience.

The solution, however, is not that simple, because African American and Wesleyan scholars often approach experience differently. One way of addressing the tension between African American and Wesleyan scholars is to borrow from feminist Sallie McFague's idea of "attention epistemology." McFague suggests that we must move from disembodied ways of knowing and doing to an embodied knowing and doing.[20] McFague is primarily focusing on ecological issues in challenging us to rethink traditional ways of knowing, but her embodied approach resonates with both African American and Wesleyan theologians. Her emphasis is on a holistic approach to knowing that is not fragmented by focusing strictly on either reason or on experience. In Wesleyan language she provides a means for integrating head, heart, and body as an approach to knowing.

This is where McFague's idea of an attention epistemology can offer a different approach without negating central theological commitments by either African American or Wesleyan theologians. She describes an attention epistemology in the following way:

> Attention epistemology is listening, paying attention to an other, the other, in itself, for itself. It is the opposite of means-ends thinking, thinking of anything, everything, as useful, necessary, pleasurable to *oneself*, that is, assuming that everything that is not the self has only utilitarian value. An attention epistemology assumes *intrinsic* value of anything, everything, that is not the self. Each and every different entity in the universe has its own (from our point of view) "pointless independent existence" and the implicit assumption, therefore, is that we can *know* others, all others, not only as human beings but "animals, birds, stones, and trees," only insofar as we pay attention to them.[21]

McFague calls for a shift from focusing on the self to really paying attention to others. An embodied knowing rethinks traditional categories (for example, universal versus particular) by shifting the focus to really listening to, and valuing, the other. This challenges both African American and Wesleyan scholars to reexamine how they use experience in relation to those within the broader Methodist family. No longer can either side be satisfied with a just-us approach to methodology because paying attention to the other becomes primary.

What McFague is suggesting is a dialogical process that incorporates insights from others into one's methodological approach. For example, Renita Weems helps contextualize biblical interpretations when she speaks to the inherent subjectivity that all interpreters bring to the text. Weems claims, "At the center of the re-formation of the field of biblical studies is the recognition that biblical interpretation is not isolated from the social and cultural values and political interests of the interpreter."[22] Paying attention to the particularities that inform our reading of a text can aid us in understanding why various individuals interpret the text differently. Weems argues for starting with the existential situation, which informs the questions, and ultimately the answers, we get from the text.

Weems's argument supports beginning with the existential situation, but it does not help us move toward a broader understanding of experience. Rebekah Miles helps us make this move within a Methodist context when she suggests, "Wesley's theology reminds Christians that even if the anthropological or cultural data points to extreme differences in human experience, we ground claims about our common experience in God's creating, restoring, and transforming grace."[23] Miles recognizes that there are cultural differences that need to be considered, but these differences do not mean we cannot move toward a broader understanding of experience. In the Methodist tradition the common thread is God's work in creating, restoring, and transforming humanity. Both African American and Wesleyan scholars are concerned with what God is doing in creation, how God has restored and continues to restore humanity—most important to both groups is God's transforming work in this world.

Moving toward a Pan-Methodist methodology means paying attention to the cultural and political interest inherent in biblical interpretation, and it means paying attention to God's creating, restoring, and transforming work. This means paying attention to those experiences informing our understanding of the biblical text and being formed into the right experience. African American scholars argue the need to begin with the particular or one's existential situation. Wesleyan scholars argue for the whole tenor of the Bible informing one's experiences so that the individual has the right experience. A Pan-Methodist approach pays attention to the insights of African American and Wesleyan scholarship in an effort to move toward an understanding of experience that recognizes existential differences while moving toward a broader understanding of God's work of restoration. This approach maintains the historic and cultural differences that African Americans and Euro-Americans have experienced within Methodism, and it opens up the possibility for being formed into new experiences because of God's restoring grace.

Two historical Methodist figures, Sojourner Truth and Frances Willard, are helpful illustrations of how a Pan-Methodist understanding of experience can be different and move toward a shared epistemology. Sojourner Truth, in a famous speech, "Ain't I a Woman?" questioned not only Euro-American society as a whole, but also Euro-American male interpretations of the biblical text. Truth comments:

> Dat man ober dar say dat womin needs to be helped into carriages and lifted ober ditches, and to hab de best place everywhar. Nobody eber helps me into carriages, or ober mud puddles, or gibs me any best place! And ain't I a woman? Look at my arm! I have ploughed, and planted, and gathered into barns, an no man could head me! And ain't I a woman? . . . Den dat little man in black dar, he say women can't have as much rights as men, 'cause Christ wan't a woman! Whar did your

> Christ come from? Whar did your Christ come from? From God and a woman! Man had nothin' to do wid Him![24]

Truth deconstructs and reconstructs traditional interpretations of the Bible based upon her experiences as an African American woman. She begins by pointing out that African American women are fully female and deserve the same treatment as Euro-American women. Truth then shifts to a critique of men (especially Euro-American men) who use the Bible to oppress women. She sarcastically asks, "Whar did your Christ come from?"[25] The answer, of course, is, "From God and a woman."[26] She deconstructs biblical interpretations that deny African American women equal rights and reconstructs the way women should interpret Christology. Truth's insights begin with the existential situation of African American women and move toward God's restoring grace in the lives of all women. Truth's words highlight how others were not paying attention to African American women in society.

Frances Willard was instrumental in the temperance movement and in arguing for women's ecclesial rights.[27] Willard, like Truth, fought for women's rights, and her primary opponents were Euro-American men who perceived her to be outside of the power structures of society and the church. Like Truth, Willard often felt ignored by others (particularly Euro-American men) in society. Laceye Warner discusses Willard's struggle with ecclesial structures during her time. Warner writes:

> Willard struggled with a call to ministry, which she discerned to include a call to preach and receive ordination. Such roles were not readily accessible to women in The Methodist Episcopal Church at the time. Willard expressed her vision for the church in a letter written to Mrs. D. L. Moody in 1877, in which she supported women as evangelists, . . . but also indicated the expansion of this role was "such that most people have not dreamed."[28]

Willard envisioned an expanding role for women in the church even during a time when she was not welcome into ordained ministry. She deconstructed current ecclesial practices by acknowledging her own call to preach. Willard reconstructs the role of the evangelist by suggesting most people have not imagined the significance of this title for women. By beginning with her existential situation, Willard is able to move toward a different vision of God's restoring grace, even though she recognizes a lot of work still needs to be done.

The just-us way of approaching these stories is for African American scholars (usually womanists) to talk about the importance of Truth and her experiences for black women. It is for Wesleyans (usually feminists) to talk about the importance of Willard and how she provides a lens to further Wesleyan scholarship. Staying true to their respective understandings of experience, the African American scholars focus on the particular and the Wesleyan scholars focus on moving toward a broader notion of experience. A Pan-Methodist approach recognizes the cultural differences of these women and how that influences the questions they raise. This approach also thinks about how the questions these women have raised move us toward a different understanding of experience grounded in the creating, restoring, and transforming work of God.

For instance, both women raise questions pertaining to men's oppression of women within society. The oppression takes different forms because African American women have the additional weight of race and class oppression. This does not negate the fact that both Truth and Willard begin with the particularity of their existential situations and raise issues that can move society toward a different understanding of experience grounded in God's grace. The struggle of these two women coming from very different contexts highlights the reality that within African American and Wesleyan theology seeds have been planted for a new methodological approach. Until we are able to stop focusing on ourselves and pay attention to others for their own sake, we will continue to make just-us decisions based solely upon our own needs.

The dialogue between African American and Wesleyan scholars is often a parallel conversation rather than an intersecting one that shifts the theological landscape. A shift within Pan-Methodism means that reading Willard without Truth is unacceptable. We can only catch a glimpse of the truth when reading both and understanding their existential situations as a lens into God's restoring grace. This should not be used as a forum to compare my oppression to your oppression, but as a space to pay attention to how others are oppressed and what this means for a Pan-Methodist methodology, which can move Methodist from just-us conversations toward a methodology that no longer is self-serving.

Justice and a Pan-Methodist Methodology

A methodological shift is necessary if Wesleyans and African American scholars are going to move forward in a way that honors the particularity of each side's theological commitments while broadening their understanding of the tradition at the same time. Truth and Willard are one example of how this shift can help us rethink what it means to engage the other and their particular experiences. For example, the splinters caused by slavery within Methodism can become a resource for reading Wesley and developing new theological insights for the broader Methodist tradition. In this particular work, soteriology is the theological lens I am suggesting as a starting point for such insights, because salvation is a common experience and goal that can help us transcend just-us positions.

Truth and Willard provide an example for how African American and Wesleyan scholars can emphasize the this-worldly side of salvation. Many African American scholars believe the experiences of blacks should be viewed from the perspective of Jesus' own experiences of oppression. More important, Jesus defines his own ministry as liberating people from oppression, and this includes social, psychological, and political bondage.[29] Truth's speech deals with these different levels of oppression, and her goal is liberating African American women from these forms of bondage.

Following Wesley, most Wesleyan scholars (for example, Kenneth J. Collins, Maddox, and Runyon) agree that salvation begins on this side and is consummated on the other side. These Wesleyan scholars nuance the way that prevenient, justifying, and sanctifying grace work, but all agree that these doctrines are essential to a Wesleyan soteriology. The goal is to become more Christlike by recovering the moral image of God. The recovery of the moral image of God means mirroring the mercy, truth, and justice of Christ. Ultimately, as one recovers the moral image of God, one's experiences are transformed and shaped by the biblical message toward a new life in Christ. Willard's vision for society was seeking this type of transformation in the lives of those she encountered.[30]

Whereas many African American scholars agree with the Wesleyan scholars who argue that salvation is a process beginning in this world with eventual consummation on the other side, the difference between African American and Wesleyan scholars who believe in a this-worldly salvation is that Wesleyans usually do not focus on the political and social content of salvation, but rather on the individual becoming more Christlike. For many African American scholars discussing the meaning of salvation, the transformation of systemic structures is privileged over personal transformation. Many African American scholars perceive Jesus as a liberator (some womanists would suggest he is an example of how to survive oppression) who comes to break down oppressive structures. Wesleyans focus on the Christ figure and the goal becomes a movement toward becoming more Christlike. Jesus as liberator focuses on Jesus coming and being with the oppressed to transform their situation, which is different from focusing on the Christ figure who takes on a universal meaning that has to do more with setting a standard for humanity. These positions are not mutually exclusive and can be interpreted in a way that rethinks Methodist soteriology. Although not usually emphasized in some Wesleyan scholarship, the recovery of the political image is a part of the Wesleyan salvation process and fits with an African American paradigm of liberation or survival. Similarly, African American scholars recognize the importance of the Christ figure not only as a bringer of hope, but also as the ultimate example of who we should become as Christians.

Considering experience within the framework of soteriology can create a shared space for African American and Wesleyan scholars to dialogue. African American scholars can talk about salvation in terms of liberation and this is not foreign to a Wesleyan perspective. Wesleyans can talk about the way of salvation including a this-worldly soteriology that is crucial to African American scholars. A soteriological focus frames the way experience can be used by both African American and Wesleyan scholars, setting the stage for a Pan-Methodist theological perspective that addresses justice issues and not just-us concerns.

A Pan-Methodist perspective also avoids claiming all experiences count, and no one experience qualifies as right. Grant helps us understand the connection between starting with particular contexts and a broader Pan-Methodist concern when she writes, "Because it is in the context of Black women's experience where the particular connects up with the universal . . . Black women share in the reality of a broader community."[31] Grant is specifically talking about African American women, but her point is that beginning with the particular does not make exploring common categories for the broader community impossible. Understanding the context out of which one's experiences are shaped is critical, but as Christians we should always be mindful of the experiences of others. Moreover, we should be mindful that God's grace is always involved in all of our human experiences. Miles argues this is not something that can be measured empirically or known with confidence because "it is a claim of faith."[32] As humans we are continually participating with God in the work of restoring and transforming society, and this requires paying attention to all that God has created.

CHAPTER 3

WESLEYAN SOTERIOLOGICAL JUST-US

Soteriology permeates many recent works in Wesleyan studies. Two common denominators in many of these soteriological works are a hermeneutic of return to the work of John Wesley and interpreting Wesleyan soteriology through the lens of the *via salutis*, the way of salvation. A return to Wesley is perceived as critical because he is the theological progenitor of the Wesleyan movement and as such provides key insights into the meaning of salvation for Methodist scholars around the globe.

As straightforward as these two common denominators are, debate continues because of different interpretations of Wesley and various understandings of *via salutis*.[1] One way of categorizing these diverse opinions within Wesleyan studies is to organize the differences into four schools of thought: those that (1) emphasize conversion, (2) emphasize a process or gradual approach to soteriology, (3) emphasize a complete renewal approach for all of creation, and (4) what I term a Wesleyan feminist soteriological perspective. Certainly there is overlap among these various positions, but each has distinct characteristics.

The Way of Salvation

Most Wesleyan scholars agree that John Wesley's soteriology includes justification, new birth, and sanctification. The debate among Wesleyan scholars is often an attempt to clarify the relationship among these three doctrines. Wesley describes justification in the following manner in a 1765 sermon, "The Scripture Way of Salvation":

> Justification is another word for pardon. It is the forgiveness of all our sins, and (what is necessarily implied therein) our acceptance with God.

> The price whereby this has been procured for us (commonly termed the "meritorious cause" of our justification) is the blood and righteousness of Christ, or (to express it a little more clearly) all that Christ has done and suffered for us till "he poured out his soul for the transgressors." The immediate effects of justification are, the peace of God, a "peace that passeth all understanding," and a "rejoicing in *hope* of the glory of God," "with *joy* unspeakable and full of glory."[2]

Wesley did not consider his understanding of justification to be radical or outside of the contours of the thinking of his day. Justification is fundamentally the pardoning of human sins, without which salvation is not possible. As Wesley's sermon title indicates, Wesley believed this understanding of justification is rooted in Scripture.

Although many Wesleyan scholars agree on the definition of justification, the picture becomes cloudier when attempts are made to explain the relationship between justification and new birth. In part, the difficulty Wesleyan scholars face is in trying to interpret the meaning and ordering of new birth within the *via salutis*. For instance, Wesley writes in a 1760 sermon, "The New Birth":

> If any doctrines within the whole compass of Christianity may be properly termed fundamental they are doubtless these two—the doctrine of justification, and that of the new birth: the former relating to that great work which God does *for us*, in forgiving our sins; the latter to the great work which God does *in us*, in renewing our fallen nature. In order of time neither of these is before the other. In the moment we are justified by the grace of God through the redemption that is in Jesus we are also "born of the Spirit"; but in order of thinking, as it is termed, justification precedes the new birth. We first conceive his wrath to be turned away, and then his Spirit to work in our hearts.[3]

Obviously this is just one of Wesley's statements about new birth within the Christian journey. Because Wesley rightly attempts to shift individuals away from linear thinking about these doctrines to a more holistic understanding, he opens up space for how one interprets the relationship between justification and new birth, with questions such as, "When are we transformed by God's grace (in justification and new birth)?" The answer varies depending on whom you ask. This is one of the reasons different schools of thought developed concerning Wesleyan soteriology.

For Wesley, justification and new birth are just a part of the soteriological landscape. Sanctification fills in the soteriological landscape and makes the picture clearer. Wesley describes sanctification in "The Scripture Way of Salvation" in these terms:

> And at the same time that we are justified, yea, in that very moment, *sanctification* begins. In that instant we are "born again," "born from above," "born of the Spirit." There is a *real* as well as a *relative* change. We are inwardly renewed by the power of God. We feel the "love of God shed abroad in our heart by the Holy Ghost which is given unto us," producing love to all mankind, and more especially to the children of God; expelling the love of the world, the love of pleasure, of ease, of honour, of money; together with pride, anger, self-will, and every other evil temper—in a word, changing the "earthly, sensual, devilish" mind into "the mind which was in Christ Jesus."[4]

For Wesley, the pardoning of one's sins (justification) is not the end-all of salvation, but one should have an expectation of real and relative change taking place in one's life.[5] The change in one's life is inward but manifests itself in outward actions.

Notice that Wesley uses the term *temper* in the above sermon as a way of helping readers better understand the inward change he is advocating. By temper, Wesley means God's ability to make enduring changes to our very being.[6] This inward change is best understood as no longer taking on the mind of the devil, but instead taking on the mind of Christ.[7] Through the working of the Holy Spirit this inward change enables one to love God and one's neighbor differently.

Justification and sanctification are constitutive components for understanding Wesleyan soteriology. Two cautions are important at this juncture regarding Wesleyan soteriology. Wesley's soteriology was contextual because he perceived himself, in part, to be continuing the tradition of the Church of England.[8] By contrast, I am suggesting that many Wesleyan scholars, by ignoring African American Methodist contributions, are not contextual enough. Wesley's understanding of soteriology is more complex than described here, but the intent is to give readers a lens into the hermeneutic of return that the different schools of thought are using to interpret Wesley.

School One: Conversion

Kenneth Collins is representative of those advocating for interpreting Wesleyan soteriology through the lens of conversion. Collins and others in the conversion camp nuance Wesleyan scholars who ignore the importance of transformation occurring in justification. The term *conjunctive* is important for Collins because it creates the balance he perceives as necessary when reading Wesley.[9] Reading Wesley conjunctively means developing the right relationship between God's initiative in prevenient grace and human response.[10]

Those favoring a conversion model also perceive the relationship between instantaneous understandings of Wesleyan soteriology and gradual approaches as conjunctive. Collins writes:

> During the 1990s works on Wesley's doctrine of salvation emerged that placed a premium on process, on gradual, incremental development, but neglected, in the eyes of some scholars, Wesley's equal emphasis on the "instantaneous" aspects of redemption. Here Wesley's well crafted conjunction of *both* gradual *and* instantaneousness was in danger of being neglected, if not out-right repudiated.[11]

For those favoring a conversion model, what is at stake is the loss of conversion as an experience of real transformation in the Wesleyan tradition. Conversion is not simply an emotional state of being experienced by a certain type of Christian, but a lens for interpreting Wesley's soteriology. Therefore, a conversion model seeks to maintain the integrity of a Wesleyan soteriological paradigm while emphasizing the importance of instantaneous conversion.

One of the ways those in this school of thought do this is by clearly defining human participation in the *via salutis*. They argue that God unilaterally converts the individual, and they minimize the role we humans play (humans are almost passive). In fact, one of the primary concerns for those in this school of thought is a more synergistic view of salvation—that it is God and humanity together working out one's salvation. Those who support a conversion model strongly disagree with synergism, arguing God acts more unilaterally in justification.[12] The significance of this point for those in the conversion school is twofold: (1) emphasis on instantaneous conversion, and (2) determining when one is justified.

The emphasis on instantaneous conversion as central to justification is best expressed by the difference between understanding Jesus as a great moral example for humanity and knowing Jesus as one's personal savior.[13] The former suggests that Jesus is one of various options for living one's life and that Jesus is something outside of one's being. Another way to think about Jesus as a great moral example is to acknowledge that one can grasp intellectually what Jesus means, without experiencing any impact upon the heart. Knowing Jesus as one's personal savior, however, suggests Jesus' actions in dying on the cross are for the individual personally. This shift in language means one believes Jesus is not just something to be understood outside of oneself, but someone who integrates holiness of heart and life.[14]

Inextricably connected to this understanding of instantaneous conversion is clearly defining when justification occurs. Justification is not a gradual process that enables individuals to continuously be convicted of their sin, but rather is a real transformation of our relationship with God.[15] John Tyson argues, "Justification is a renewed relationship with God in which a person *realizes* that he or she is pardoned, forgiven, loved, and accepted by God."[16] The key point for those within the conversion school is that real transformation occurs when one is justified.

If real transformation occurs in justification, then what difference does this make for understanding Wesley's soteriology? Collins argues it prevents the severing of justification from new birth. He writes: "The separation of justification from the new birth almost invariably leads to the kind of antinomianism which Wesley impugned throughout his career. For although it is true that only sinners are justified, one cannot *remain* under the power of sin, typical of the faith of a servant, and yet be justified."[17]

Collins' point is Wesley did not sever the relationship between justification and new birth the way some Wesleyan scholars have done in recent times (for example, those who emphasize a process approach to soteriology). Claiming to be converted means one recognizes God's pardoning work (justification) and the work of the Holy Spirit in a person (new birth) as transforming one's life at that moment. Conversionists believe this does not negate the importance of continuing to grow into the mind of Christ (sanctification) because justification or conversion is both instantaneous and gradual. It does negate severing the relationship between justification and new birth in a way that blurs God acting unilaterally in the life of a sinner.

Although those supporting a conversion model differ from a gradualist Wesleyan soteriological approach to the relationship between justification and new birth, they do tend to agree with gradualists on the importance of loving God and one's neighbor. For all Christians, loving God and loving one's neighbor are fundamental. The two approaches still will differ on what loving God and one's neighbor means theologically, because of their perspectives of justification. Those supporting a conversion model believe it is only when one is justified that a renewed relationship occurs with God.[18] This does not mean there is not a relationship with God prior, but that the relationship has been radically transformed.

Theologically, this implies that an individual who is not justified can misinterpret the act of loving one's neighbor. Tyson describes the difference in the following manner: "Prior to Aldersgate, Wesley already had in place a highly developed doctrine of sanctification, an appreciation for the necessity of obedience and active love of neighbor. After Aldersgate, he did not forget about sanctification but came to see the obligation to do good works as the necessary fruit of faith rather than its origin."[19] Loving one's neighbor is important regardless of whether one is truly justified, but for those within the conversion camp it is only after justification that the act of loving one's neighbor is done as a fruit of one's renewed relationship with God.

Although a lot more can be stated, there are three points that need to be considered in light of Pan-Methodism. First, it cannot be underscored enough that the framework of this model most resembles the actual experience of slaves and free blacks in the late 1700s (continuing into the 1800s) who became Methodist. This implies that many African Americans experienced a conversion type of soteriology, which emphasized Jesus as their personal savior. In theological language, this means the pardoning of sin and the ongoing working of the Holy Spirit were critical components of the way many African Americans who "converted" during that time understood salvation. Therefore, congruencies exist between those supporting a conversion model and early African American expressions of salvation.

Second, unfortunately those supporting a conversion model do not go far enough in contextualizing Wesleyan soteriology because they fail to fully engage African American Methodism. It is at this point that those favoring conversion fail to do what Wesley did in England by contextualizing their Wesleyan theology for many Methodists in the United States. This is not to say that they have ignored the subject completely.[20] It would be more fair to say that the way in which Wesley is contextualized in the United States largely ignores the insights of African American Methodism, even though American Methodism was developed within a racial arena. For example, a conversion model would greatly benefit by exploring the relationship between justification and new birth within

Pan-Methodism as a way to understand Wesleyan soteriology and its viability within this context.

Third, those supporting a conversion model for soteriology emphasize a personal relationship with Jesus based upon his death and resurrection. Tyson points out Wesley's shift in language from talking about Jesus in general to claiming Jesus as his personal savior who died on the cross for him.[21] The life of Jesus and his position in society are not portrayed as significant at all in the language used by conversionists, who continually emphasize a personal relationship with Jesus based upon the cross. In an effort to protect instantaneous conversion, the life of Jesus and its meaning for the oppressed get downplayed. In other words, inward change is emphasized, and outward actions, especially social action, are downplayed. Contextualizing their model to be more inclusive of Pan-Methodism would serve as a corrective to this shortcoming and would also open up a dialogue on the meaning of Jesus' life as constitutive to conversion.

School Two: Wesleyan Soteriology as a Process

Randy Maddox is representative of the Wesleyan soteriology understood more gradually. This school within Wesleyan scholarship emphasizes a gradual recovery of the moral image of God, meaning that instantaneous conversion gets downplayed. Maddox describes the process of Wesleyan soteriology as "intertwined facets of an overarching purpose—our gradual recovery of the holiness that God has always intended for us."[22] Whereas those advocating a gradual model agree with those favoring a conversion model about the theological framework of Wesleyan soteriology, they differ on how the frame is constructed. Maddox describes in the following paragraph how new birth gets misinterpreted within Wesley's soteriology:

> There are few places where the typical Reformed *ordo salutis* differs more from Wesley's understanding of the Way of Salvation than the issue of regeneration. Reformed Scholastics equated regeneration in the most proper sense with the New Birth, which is God's gracious gift that instantaneously and irresistibly transforms sinners from their fallen

> state—in which they are incapable of good works, faith, or even repentance—to a new life where repentance and faith are natural.[23]

It is obvious in reading this paragraph that those advocating a gradual model interpret Wesley differently than those favoring conversion. Maddox challenges three important conversionist claims: (1) God's unilateral role in justification and new birth, (2) the emphasis on sinners moving from one state of being to another, and (3) the place of good works in the soteriological process. Certainly the differences pointed out between gradualists and conversionists are important, but we should not lose sight of the fact that these two schools agree more than they disagree. The focus here is on nuances between gradualists and conversionists that ultimately impact contextualizing Wesley into a Pan-Methodist soteriology.

The issue of the role of God in the salvation process is an important difference that needs further illumination. Those advocating a gradual approach to Wesleyan soteriology agree with conversionists that God acting first is necessary. The difference is on the human side of the equation; gradualists believe that God and humans work cooperatively. Maddox calls this relationship between God and humans *responsible grace*.[24] He defines responsible grace in the following way: "I discerned in Wesley's work an abiding concern to preserve the vital tension between two truths that he viewed as co-definitive of Christianity: without God's grace, we *cannot* be saved; while without our (grace-empowered, but uncoerced) participation, God's grace *will not* save."[25]

A gradualist approach suggests that humans are active in the entire soteriological process because of prevenient grace. Humans are not acting in place of God and only can respond to God's action, but humans are active. In contrast, a conversionist approach to Wesleyan soteriology suggests it is only after one is properly justified and experiences new birth that a real human response to God is possible. The difference between gradualists and conversionists hinges on how one reads the human response to prevenient grace. Is the human response to prevenient grace such that there is a synergistic relationship between God and humans, which conversionists will not support? Might they instead understand the human response to prevenient grace as more in line with an awareness of God, maintaining that it is still God alone who acts in justification and new birth? The intent here is not to resolve these issues, but to help illuminate the differences within these Wesleyan schools of thought.

A second difference is that the gradual model shifts from emphasizing instantaneous conversion to a more protracted soteriological experience that emphasizes "intensifying degrees"[26] throughout the salvation process. Shifting the focus to intensifying degrees of grace changes the way justification, and especially new birth, are perceived within Wesleyan soteriology. Maddox rhetorically asks, "So which of these—New Birth or sanctification—should most properly be identified as 'regeneration'?"[27] The answer is both, because they represent intensifying degrees of regeneration.[28]

The reason regeneration is identified both with new birth and sanctification is that gradualists interpret Wesley not only through a forensic lens, but also a therapeutic one. The emphasis switches from focusing on God pardoning humanity to include the Eastern focus of therapeutic transformation.[29] This shift in emphasis means Wesley is interpreted differently and no longer is read strictly through a Western forensic lens. Maddox argues: "Western understandings of salvation have focused more on the legal act of pardon, which can be a momentary transaction. While many of these traditions have allowed a place for gradual sanctification in the Christian life, they have typically been careful to subsume this growth to the act of justification."[30]

Gradualists believe Wesley's soteriology is unique because it does not subsume a therapeutic understanding of salvation under a more forensic interpretation of justification. A therapeutic understanding of salvation borrows more from the Eastern tradition of healing sickness, and a forensic interpretation of salvation borrows from the Western tradition of guilt. Therefore, a gradual model shifts Wesleyan soteriology from emphasizing a "momentary transaction" (forensic interpretation) that enables one to move to a new state of being (not guilty) and focuses on intensifying degrees of transformation.

What is at stake for gradualists is the role of justification in Wesleyan soteriology. By arguing for a gradual model of salvation, justification and new birth get diluted in comparison to a conversionist understanding of Wesleyan soteriology. In the opinion of gradualists, what is gained is that individuals no longer believe justification signals the ending of all transformation within the Christian journey.[31] An individual must continue to grow into holiness, and this is better expressed as a gradual process. This is not to say that gradualists ignore instantaneous transitions, but rather they perceive in the mature Wesley an emphasis on the gradual work of salvation.

A third difference between gradualists and conversionists is the nuanced interpretation between the two schools of what loving one's neighbor means for Wesleyan soteriology. The difference in this instance between gradualists and conversionists is the place for good works within the Christian journey. Gradualists will differ from conversionists on their understanding of good works within the Christian journey because the fruit produced by one's faith is not dependent upon a strict forensic definition of justification.

As noted earlier, conversionists believe there is a difference between good works done prior to when one was justified and good works done after one is justified. This difference hinges on their understanding that real transformation occurs in justification. Gradualists obscure the picture a little more because the transformation occurring is not a moment of moving from one state to another, but rather a process of intensifying degrees of growth. Thus, it is the process itself that is transformative, and claiming one moment as definitive is more difficult.

The result is that loving one's neighbor no longer hinges on justification. Loving one's neighbor is a lifelong process transforming one's tempers to becoming more Christlike.[32] This shift is more theological than it is practical, but the implications are important. If one completely adheres to the gradual model of Wesleyan soteriology, then it suggests, if taken to the extreme, that one's relationship with God and neighbor can always be a work in progress with no definitive moment for claiming real transformation. Conversely, a conversionist approach, if taken to the extreme, always has a definitive moment of transformation that enables an individual to know that their relationship with God and neighbor has been radically transformed. Although neither model seeks to live in the extremes, it does emphasize their different concerns.

It is important for a Pan-Methodist soteriology to note that a gradualist model shares less with current African American theology than the other two models in this chapter because it does not emphasize conversion (the model for many in the black church) and it does not point toward liberation (the model for many African Americans in the academy). Because a gradualist approach focuses on degrees of difference, it lends itself to various theological interpretations depending on the lens one brings to the model.

For example, focusing on degrees of difference is a strength of the gradualist approach, if one interprets the gradualist understanding of the salvation process as more synergistic. The issue is how one interprets grace.

If God and humans are in a synergistic relationship in which God takes the intiative and humans are enabled to respond, then it opens up the possibility of salvation for all of humanity. A conversionist model can be read as suggesting humans are so passive in the salvation process that God almost "irresistibly" saves people. A synergistic understanding of salvation protects against irresistible grace being used as a means of preselecting some against others, certainly a just-us understanding of soteriology.

The danger of irresistible grace for African Americans within the American context is Euro-Americans are preselected by God and African Americans are not.[33] The logic of irresistible grace is God favors some over others. The problem with this logic within the American context is God almost always favors Euro-Americans. This logic developed as a result of slavery. A synergistic understanding of salvation theologically avoids the idea of preselection, because salvation is a process worked out in relationship with God and humanity. Gradualists are not claiming God and humans are equal partners in this relationship, because, following Wesley, they protect the primacy of God acting first.[34] God acting first carries with it an expectation of human responsibility to participate in the salvation process.[35] The remaining difficulty is, of course, determining what is meant by humanity's response to God.

A weakness of the gradualist approach in light of Pan-Methodism can be found in its primary focus on the recovery of the moral image of God. Gradualists are not arguing that the recovery of the moral image of God is one-dimensional, because they perceive it as an inward change resulting in outward transformation. Maddox clarifies this point when he writes:

> Wesley's description of Christian salvation as a therapy of the soul might suggest that he limited human salvation to an internal spiritual sphere of life. Given his understanding of the role of the affections or tempers in human action, he certainly assumed that this is where authentic salvation or holiness is grounded. Yet (like the early Greek theologians) Wesley insisted throughout his life that salvation must involve not only inner holiness but also the recovery of actual moral righteousness in our outward lives.[36]

Maddox's point is that Wesley's understanding of salvation was more than just an inward change that never translated into any outward difference in a person's life. In fact, a real inward change means our outward lives will be different.

The weakness of this position is it continues focusing on the personal, and the social is a by-product of personal transformation. A gradualist approach suggests that the direction of change is from inward to outward. It is not until one is changed on the inside that one can begin to change those relationships on the outside, and the implication is that personal transformation gets privileged. Social change may occur if enough changed people are working toward a common goal, but social change is not the emphasis of a gradualist approach to Wesleyan soteriology. In part, this is a result of gradualists not fully incorporating the recovery of the political image into their soteriology. Limiting Wesleyan soteriology primarily to the recovery of the moral image emphasizes the personal and de-emphasizes the social.

By moral image, Wesley meant the recovery of love, mercy, and justice in one's life. The problem is that Wesleyan scholars usually articulate the recovery of the moral image in personal language, which leaves open the issue of social oppression. One place where social oppression can be addressed is in the recovery of the political image, which focuses on stewardship, but gradualists do not make this move. They recognize the recovery of the political image as part of moving toward Christlikeness, but do not articulate its importance for the American context.

For African Americans, and specifically African American Methodists, this means the structures of oppression in the United States primarily get addressed at the personal level. A gradualist model has little to offer in terms of deconstructing social sin, and there seem to be few soteriological implications of doing so within the United States. This does not mean that a gradualist approach ignores the oppression of African Americans in the United States, but rather that its Wesleyan model of soteriology is inadequate to address structural sin.

School Three: Complete Renewal

Ted Runyon is representative of the complete renewal school of thought for Wesleyan soteriology. The complete renewal model has affinity with the gradual model, but differs from it in the way that creation and eschatology are emphasized as central components. A complete renewal model does not simply focus on the recovery of the moral image, but also emphasizes the recovery of the political image. Gradualists name the political image of God as an important aspect of Wesleyan soteriology, but primarily focus on the recovery of the moral image for Wesleyan theology. By integrating the political image into their soteriology, those advocating for a complete renewal model open up new possibilities for contextualization beyond eighteenth-century England.

A complete renewal model does not share the same Wesleyan soteriological commitments as a conversion model because of the way it understands salvation. If God's pardoning of humanity becomes the central focus for salvation, then defining salvation as justification is appropriate.[37] A complete renewal model seeks to expand this definition of salvation to include "what God's forgiveness aims to accomplish" in life.[38] While not negating the importance of justification, this model expands the goal of salvation in such a way that Wesleyan soteriology is a lifetime pursuit.[39] A conversionist approach is more complex than simply arguing for pardon, but the real distinction between conversionist and complete renewal is the latter's expansion of how we define salvation to include the goal of forgiveness—renewal of creation.

In part, Wesleyan soteriology is a lifetime pursuit because God's work of renewing creation is ongoing. A complete renewal approach suggests that reading Wesleyan soteriology through a creation lens gets at the heart of Wesley's theology and provides cues for how we can shift our thinking on salvation today. Runyon describes in the following manner the importance of using creation as the lens to interpret Wesleyan soteriology:

> The cosmic drama of the renewing of creation begins, therefore, with the renewal of the *imago Dei* in humankind. This is the indispensable key to Wesley's whole soteriology. Despite the importance in his own experience of Luther's doctrine of justification by faith mediated to him by the Moravians, Wesley distanced himself from their identification of salvation with justification alone, insisting that the "great salvation" cannot stop short of a renewal of that original vocation for which humanity was created, to live as the image of God in the world.[40]

In the above quotation Runyon both differentiates a complete renewal approach from the other two schools of thought and sets the parameters for reinterpreting Wesleyan soteriology through the lens of creation. He differentiates a complete renewal approach from the conversionist approach by claiming that Wesley eventually moves away from emphasizing justification alone; and he differentiates it from the gradualist approach in the way he connects justification, new birth, and sanctification, using creation as the theological glue. Therefore, the keys to understanding a complete renewal approach are interpreting Wesleyan soteriology using the doctrine of creation and expanding what is meant by the recovery of the *imago dei.*

A complete renewal approach begins with creation because it assumes God not only transforms humanity but also the entire world, to live out God's original intent for it.[41] The goal of salvation is not simply new creatures but a new creation. A complete renewal model sets the stage for this interpretation by quoting from Wesley's sermon, "The General Spread of the Gospel," where Wesley writes:

> God is already renewing the face of the earth. And we have strong reason to hope that the work he hath begun he will carry on unto the day of his Lord Jesus; that he will never intermit this blessed work of his spirit until he has fulfilled all his promises; until he hath put a period to sin and misery, and infirmity, and death; and re-established universal holiness and happiness, and caused all the inhabitants of the earth to sing together, "Hallelujah! The Lord God omnipotent reigneth! . . . Blessing, glory and wisdom, and honour, and power, and might be unto our God for ever and ever!"[42]

Those advocating for a complete renewal model interpret the theological implications in the above Wesley quotation as the starting point for developing a Wesleyan soteriology that shifts the focus away from justification alone. It alters thinking about Wesleyan soteriology from beginning with the death and resurrection of Jesus the Christ to God's plan for humanity originating in creation. This is a dramatic change because it means the work of salvation started even before Jesus' death and resurrection.

This move means personal and social salvation are held together in a creative tension. The complete renewal model does not negate the emphasis by conversionists and gradualists of growing into Christlikeness. The difference is that, by holding creation and eschatology together, a complete renewal approach more clearly defines the social aspect of sanctification for Wesleyan soteriology. Runyon proposes, "The renewed image is a witness in society, a reflection to others of God's own loving care, and therefore can accomplish the purposes to which God calls it only in a social context."[43] Growing into Christlikeness is a part of God's intent for creation and includes a social dimension not as clearly defined in the other two schools.

A right relationship with God is more than becoming morally upright (that is, the recovery of the moral image), it also means actively reconstituting humanity's role for stewardship in creation (recovery of the political image).[44] This is a synergistic relationship between God and humanity. Runyon describes it in the following manner:

> A new creation! From Wesley's standpoint, this is the *sine qua non*. If humanity is to become different from what it is now in its grasping and greedy attempts to produce its own security, what is needed is transcendent resources, partnership with and participation in the divine Spirit, that *synergy* (working together) which is a partnership in which the Creator informs, infuses, and inspires the creature with the original goal of human existence.[45]

Describing synergy in this way both challenges and agrees with conversionists and gradualists. It challenges conversionists because, like the gradualist position, it claims that God and humanity are actively engaged throughout the salvation process. Yet, it challenges gradualists because creation becomes the lens for understanding synergy, meaning human participation in the salvation process is based upon God's original intent for creation and not centered only on christological issues.

It challenges both conversionists and gradualists because the synergistic relationship proposed in a complete renewal model emphasizes the recovery of the political image of God. A right relationship with God is more than just personal; it also includes reconstituting humanity's role in creation.[46] Conversionists and gradualists include the political image as part of their understanding of the recovery of the image of God but do not develop it as part of the soteriological process like many advocating for a complete renewal model. The idea of synergy gets expanded in the way a renewal approach integrates recovery of the political image of God with recovery of the moral image.

It is fair to suggest that a complete renewal approach to soteriology also may agree with conversionists to the extent that God acts in creation to "infuse humanity," almost making humans passive in the process. The human response, however, is shifted from forensic issues to responding to God's original intent for creation. In other words, a complete renewal model and conversionists agree on human passivity to a point, but they differ on when God infuses humanity for salvific purposes. A complete renewal approach is not incompatible with a gradualist approach if one reads both models as inferring that God's intent for humanity is linked to creation. The difficulty with making this claim for gradualists is that their interpretation of Wesleyan soteriology does not make the creative move, so central to the complete renewal model, of using creation as their lens.

The complete renewal model in many ways is the most creative of the three Wesleyan soteriological approaches because it not only interprets Wesley but contextualizes Wesley for the contemporary United States. Loving God and loving one's neighbor takes on a contextual emphasis that integrates God's original intent for all of creation. For instance, we can rethink today's ecological concerns by understanding our role as God's stewards of creation and what this entails in terms of our neighbors.[47] As Americans we are not free to consume and use a greater percentage of the world's resources just to make our lives more comfortable. Loving one's neighbor requires mirroring God's governance for all of creation, and this is what we are called to do in relation to our neighbors.[48]

A complete renewal model shifts loving one's neighbor from a strictly moral practice to include political practices.[49] This redefines loving one's neighbor not only as a personal commitment but also as a social concern. One has to be careful not to confuse "social" to mean any issue that someone or some group feels deserves a hearing. For example, displaying the Ten Commandments at a public building is a social concern but not necessarily a soteriological issue; because whether the commandments are displayed is not directly related to God's intent for humanity in creation. Certainly, living out the commandments is a soteriological concern of great importance, but simply displaying the commandments is not instrumental to God's intent for humanity in creation. A complete renewal approach emphasizes understanding Wesleyan soteriology through the lens of creation as it pertains to God's intent for creation, and loving one's neighbor is a result of this intent.

Because a complete renewal model uses creation as a lens for interpreting Wesleyan soteriology, it develops a healthier tension between personal and social salvation, which makes it more congruent with the thinking of some African American liberation scholars. Both the conversion and gradual models focus primarily on personal salvation, which renders their constructive analysis to structural oppression inadequate. A complete renewal model does not negate personal salvation as it develops a constructive approach for thinking about structural sin. Runyon makes this claim about a healthy tension between personal and social salvation:

> It is an important corrective to the evangelical Protestant tendency to equate salvation with justification or conversion, for it points to the

> divine goal not just of reconciliation and a new status in the eyes of God, but the gracious re-creation of both individuals and the social world through the renewal of the image of God in humanity. It holds out the promise that through the transforming energy of divine love reflected into the world the future can indeed surpass the present.[50]

By arguing for the re-creation of "individuals and the social world," a complete renewal model opens up Wesleyan soteriology in a way that no longer de-emphasizes structural sin. For African American Methodism this means that ending the oppression blacks face in the United States is a part of God's salvific plan of renewal. If God's intent in creation was harmony and love among all of creation, then ending structural oppression is a part of the renewal of creation. A complete renewal approach builds a bridge in moving toward a Pan-Methodist theology because it opens up Wesleyan soteriology to include a constructive means of thinking about social salvation.

A complete renewal model, however, does not go far enough in its contextualization of Wesleyan soteriology. For example, ecological concerns are usually described in terms of global warming, American consumption, and so on. Rarely discussed is the impact of ecological issues on minorities, and especially on poor people of color. James Cone argues:

> The logic that led to slavery and segregation in the Americas, colonization and apartheid in Africa, and the rule of white supremacy throughout the world is the same one that leads to the exploitation of animals and the ravaging of nature. It is a mechanistic and instrumental logic that defines everything and everybody in terms of their contribution to the development and defense of white supremacy. People who fight against white racism but fail to connect it to the degradation of the earth are anti-ecological—whether they know it or not. People who struggle against environmental degradation but do not incorporate in it a disciplined and sustained fight against white supremacy are racists—whether they acknowledge it or not. The fight for justice cannot be segregated but must be integrated with the fight for life in all its forms.[51]

Cone points out that fighting for justice is an integrated endeavor that involves all forms of oppression. The problem with a complete renewal model is that one can focus on environmental concerns in the United States but miss how environmental issues are related to oppression. I am not suggesting that this is the intent of a complete renewal model, but unless one intentionally interprets issues through a structural oppression lens, as Cone does, in many cases the contextualization stops with just the African American community. While a complete renewal approach builds a bridge toward Pan-Methodism, it still falls short of the contextualization necessary for truly engaging African American Methodism.

Wesleyan Feminist Soteriology

It is important to recognize the contributions of Wesleyan feminists to Wesleyan soteriology. A few clarifications, however, are necessary. First, Wesleyan feminists continue to experience just-us within Wesleyan studies, and this is evident, in part, given the deficit of material published on this topic. Second, one should not consider all feminism to be the same, meaning that the classification of Wesleyan feminism in this book does not fully distinguish the various forms of Wesleyan feminism. For example, Susie C. Stanley considers herself a biblical feminist but differentiates her understanding of feminism from others.[52] Third, the goal in this section is to highlight some of the work done by Wesleyan feminists who are rethinking Wesleyan soteriology in creative ways.

Catherine Keller, in an article entitled "Salvation Flows: Eschatology for a Feminist Wesleyanism," suggests some connections between Wesleyan soteriology and feminism. Her lens for reading Wesley has affinity with the complete renewal approach to Wesleyan soteriology. Keller writes: "I interpret Wesley's symbol of the *new creation* by means of his radical innovation of *soteriology*. For in John Wesley's edgiest soteriological insight—that of the saving synergy of divine grace and human response—lies the sympathy between feminism and Wesleyanism. From it flows the potential for a vital Wesleyan future."[53] Keller's focus is on the synergistic relationship between God and humanity because she seeks to avoid images of divine power that make humanity inactive in the soteriological process.[54] Redefining God's power in this manner has implications for recovering the political image of God.

If we interpret God's power as only masculine and controlling, then this is what gets mirrored to the world and will constitute our stewardship within creation. Redefining God's power to be more participatory and less controlling can create an image of mutuality that moves away from "unilateral sovereignty."[55] The recovery of the political image of God continues to be thwarted as long as we imagine and live out God's power as controlling. The disenfranchised always end up on the bottom in this model, with power flowing from the top down. What Keller proposes turns this model sideways by arguing Wesleyan soteriology is best understood from the perspective of an invitation into agency and not the loss of agency.[56]

Keller's proposal differs drastically from a conversionist approach, which seeks to protect the sovereignty of God. While a conversionist approach is not suggesting humans are not a part of the salvation process, it is careful to emphasize the unilateral work of God in justification and new birth. The danger conversionists perceive in claiming a synergistic relationship throughout the soteriological process is the insinuation that humanity saves itself. Keller's approach also differs from a gradualist or complete renewal model. She writes:

> Here let me suggest that rather than try to reconcile the free synergy of grace with a totalizing recreation, we consistently interpret Wesley's new creation in terms of his soteriology. In other words, we need not adopt the literalist interpretation of the biblical new creation as an absolute finality. No matter how perfect, beautiful, and joyful is the restoration, if it *finally* overrides the agency of the creature and its capacity to respond in love, then the reconstitution is *a work not of love but of dominance.*[57]

Keller's version of Wesleyan feminism seeks to divorce Wesley's understanding of the new creation from eschatology and connect it to soteriology.[58] She does this because she fears a complete renewal model moves toward a universalist eschatology that circles around and becomes another form of dominance. She reads Wesleyan eschatology as promoting a beautiful ending for creation; but this ending turns into another form of domination because humans have no ultimate say in the process. By divorcing eschatology from soteriology, Keller avoids developing a soteriological approach that ends in another form of domination, and she maintains human freedom throughout the process.

Keller's approach to Wesleyan soteriology focuses on deconstructing unilateral sovereignty because she is interested in reimagining the power relationships we as humans live out with one another. Loving one's neighbor involves not only a moral shift but a political shift as well. Similar to a complete renewal model, recovering the political image of God is central to reconstituting one's relationship with God and neighbor. The difference in their approaches to the recovery of the political image is that a complete renewal model maintains the connection of eschatology to soteriology.

The strength of Keller's approach is its creativity in rethinking Wesleyan salvation by divorcing soteriology from eschatology. Keller is able to redefine both the vertical and horizontal power relationships that we live out when we love God and love our neighbors. The challenge, however, to Keller's approach is that God ultimately lacks the power to act independently. Because of the baggage associated with masculinity, Keller is willing to relinquish traditional models of God's power in favor of a God who is invitational but not coercive.

Many African American scholars, particularly liberationists, are uncomfortable with redefining God's power to Keller's extreme. While agreeing with Keller on the importance of God's power not being coercive, these scholars are unwilling to relinquish God's ultimate authority to judge humanity. In fact, Keller runs the risk of putting God in the same box she seeks to avoid because God's power is so connected to humanity that determining the difference between the two can be confusing. In order to deconstruct systemic racism, defining God's power is important, and clearly differentiating God's ultimate authority from humanity is necessary.

Although not all Wesleyan feminists think about Wesleyan soteriology in the same manner, Susie Stanley and Laceye Warner agree with Keller on the importance of deconstructing theological perspectives elevating masculine power stereotypes to be equated with God's power, but they do not interpret mutuality in the same way. Stanley coins the term "egalitarian primitivism" to describe what she means by mutuality.[59] For Stanley, mutuality is based upon the biblical precept that the Holy Spirit empowers and gifts both men and women for public ministry.[60]

Stanley's understanding of soteriology focuses on men and women working together to live out what it means to recover the moral image of God. She differs from Keller because her focus is not on developing a synergistic relationship between God and humanity. In fact, by reading between the lines, one figures out quickly she agrees more with the conversionists, who seek to protect the sovereignty of God. Her feminist understanding of Wesleyan soteriology is concerned with power, but it is the power of the Holy Spirit working both in men and women to bring about changes in society.

Warner is a historian who integrates Wesleyan theology into the lives of women, especially Methodist women. She focuses on the lives, writings, and works of these women to develop her Wesleyan soteriological perspective. Moreover, Warner's approach develops an understanding of the *via salutis* that often focuses on inward transformation leading to outward change.[61] She differs from Keller because eschatology is not divorced from her soteriological insights, and God's sovereignty is central in the stories of some of the women she studies.

For example, Warner depicts Julia Foote, an African American female preacher, as being strongly influenced by the holiness movement and God's gift of entire sanctification.[62] Foote's understanding of God's power is not synergistic (Foote, while supporting humans participating with God, would still seek to protect God's sovereignty) in the manner that Keller describes it because of her interpretation of justification, but she did believe one had to respond to God's urgings.[63] The inward change Foote experiences empowers her to work for social transformation, especially related to race issues. Warner's approach to Wesleyan soteriology is helpful because we read in the stories of the women the challenges they faced in loving their neighbor. Foote persevered on her Christian journey even though she continuously encountered racial incidents that could hinder how she loved her neighbor.[64] Warner suggests that all of the women she researched learned to truly love their neighbor because they were both formed by and lived into God's salvific plan for humanity.[65] For Warner, the women she researched fractured and crossed barriers, giving us practical examples of how to make love active in Wesleyan soteriology.

Although I applaud Wesleyan feminists for doing creative work and doing a better job of integrating African Methodist resources into their scholarship, these perspectives are not beyond critique.[66] For example, I resonate strongly with Warner's approach because she does excellent integrative work, but her conclusion on racial justice and reconciliation leaves unclear the role Euro-Americans should play in this process.[67] First, it would be helpful if she better described what she means by reconciliation between the races and how her research gives us clues for moving in this direction today. Leaving open what reconciliation means, allows the church and specifically Methodists to continue practicing just-us by defining reconciliation on Eurocentric terms.

Just-us: Loving Ourselves

This chapter has outlined four approaches to Wesleyan soteriology and highlighted some of the strengths and weaknesses of each one. A common theme in all of the approaches is the importance of loving God and loving one's neighbor. This theme is the practical component of any Wesleyan soteriology approach. The challenge, however, all of these approaches face is the part of the text reading "as you love yourself." This comes at the very end of the text, but within the American context these words are important.

If Euro-Americans live out the words "as you love yourself" literally, then it means they continue to buy into the systemic whiteness permeating American culture. Love of self within the American context gets interpreted through Eurocentric religious and cultural values. In theory, a Wesleyan soteriological approach fights against loving one's self in a selfish manner because it emphasizes recovering the image of God. The problem, however, is it is hard for many Euro-Americans to move beyond systemic constructs of whiteness that influence their understanding of the *imago dei*. I am suggesting that within American Methodism the recovery of the *imago dei*, and particularly of the political image of God, is tainted because of an underlying assumption of whiteness. Cone articulates the point in this manner:

> The inability of American theology to define human nature in the light of the Oppressed One and of particular oppressed peoples stems from its identity with the structures of white power. The human person in American theology is George Washington, Thomas Jefferson, and Abraham Lincoln rolled into one and polished up a bit.[68]

Cone's point is that in the United States when we talk about image (whether it is for humans or God), most people immediately create an image that resembles the "best of whiteness." Therefore, when Wesleyan scholars emphasize the recovery of the *imago dei*, they end up perpetuating systemic whiteness, because love of one's self really means love of Eurocentricity.

Some Wesleyan scholars will argue that this critique is too harsh and unfounded given Wesley's ethical stance toward slavery and other justice issues during his life. The critique, however, is not against Wesley but against current American Methodism, specifically its Eurocentric just-us practices toward African Americans. This is why in the nineteenth century many North Euro-American Methodists could oppose slavery but still treat African Americans as second-class citizens. Loving oneself within the American context often gets translated into a descending chain of being, with whiteness at the top and blackness at the bottom. Although Northern whites opposed the institution of slavery because it went against universal principles of humanity, many did not treat African Americans as true neighbors because of prevailing assumptions surrounding whiteness and blackness.

Cone proposes:

> Oppressors are ardent lovers of humanity. They can love all persons in general, even black persons, because intellectually they can put blacks in the category called Humanity. With this perspective they can participate in civil rights and help blacks purely on the premise that they are part of a universal category. But when it comes to dealing with particular blacks, statistics transformed into black encounter, they are at a loss.[69]

Loving one's neighbor as a universal human requires no contact or transformation by an oppressor. To truly love one's neighbor when you come face-to-face with that person requires loving oneself in a transformed manner. Wesleyan scholars have to rethink Wesleyan soteriology within the United States to reflect a love of neighbor that moves beyond universal categories or simply categories that continue to perpetuate whiteness. If the theory of Wesleyan soteriology is going to be lived out in practical ways by a broader Methodist community in the United States, then Wesleyan scholars must address the systemic issue of whiteness permeating Wesley's theme of love.

CHAPTER 4

AFRICAN AMERICAN SOTERIOLOGICAL JUST-US

Black and womanist theologies continue to develop soteriological perspectives that address the reality of black life in the United States. Two common denominators in many of these perspectives are a return to black sources and the belief that Jesus' life and ministry are an integral part of the salvation process. Many African American scholars use slave narratives, literature, and other black resources, which white theologians have ignored, as a lens for understanding soteriology in the lives of black Americans. Many of these scholars also integrate Jesus' life and ministry into their soteriological perspective because of the particularity of Jesus becoming incarnate as one of the oppressed.

African American soteriological perspectives are contextual to the United States in ways that several Wesleyan studies are not because of the starting point of these disciplines. Wesleyan scholars begin with a context outside of the United States and attempt to adapt a Wesleyan perspective to our situation. The goal is to provide further insights into the importance of a contextual soteriology by focusing on three schools of thought: (1) the liberationist school, which continues to frame many black theological discussions; (2) the reconciliation school of thought, which is within a black liberation stream but resonates more with many Euro-American scholars; and (3) the survivalist school, which was developed as a womanist response to a black liberation model. The strength of these models is their attention to the actual lived reality of black Americans. My critique of the liberationist and survivalist approaches is that the biblical models that undergird these positions rely on complete physical separation from the oppressor, which is not possible in the United States. At the other end of the spectrum, proponents for reconciliation often fall into a trap of not providing enough separation between the races, given the history of oppression in America. Before analyzing the three schools of thought it is important to frame the interplay between personal and social salvation within African American soteriology.

Interplay: Personal and Social Salvation

The horrors of slavery that many Africans experienced, and especially the intentional devastation of communities, cannot be underscored enough. Africans brought to the United States as slaves were stripped of language, family, and all other communal ties to their heritage.[1] The goal was to make docile slaves who completely obeyed their masters. Slave owners tried to control every aspect of a slave's life so that slaves would accept their fate—bondage. When the Great Awakening started spreading across the country and some slaves were converted, many slave owners feared that their slaves would seek freedom.[2] Slave owners and other supporters of slavery were willing to allow slaves to be converted only if it did not destroy the institution of slavery. This meant Methodists, Baptists, and other denominations often preached a conversion that supported the structural existence of slavery while defining freedom in individualistic, otherworldly language; so the emphasis of the conversion message in theological language focused on inward change and regeneration.[3] Inward change meant no longer sinning and accepting Jesus as one's personal savior. Inward change was not usually connected to the outward transformation of society because there was fear of the destruction of the slave system.

Certainly defining freedom as an inward change not affecting the slave's physical or social condition helped engender a more individualistic strand of Christianity within the African American community. Simplifying freedom in this way, however, misses the complexity of this term for African American Christians. Christian slaves worked with polyvalent understandings of freedom because they defined it differently than those keeping them in bondage. C. Eric Lincoln and Lawrence Mamiya write this about the word *freedom* in African American religious culture:

> Throughout black history the term "freedom" has found a deep religious resonance in the lives and hopes of African Americans. Depending upon the time and the context, the implications of freedom were derived from the nature of the exigency. During slavery it meant release from bondage; after emancipation it meant the right to be educated, to

> be employed, and to move about freely from place to place. In the twentieth century freedom means social, political, and economic justice. From the very beginning of the black experience in America, one critical denotation of freedom has remained constant: freedom has always meant the absence of any restraint which might compromise one's responsibility to God.[4]

Lincoln and Mamiya describe the importance of freedom for African Americans and the different connotations this word has taken on since slavery. Although many Africans were indoctrinated into an understanding of freedom that suited their oppressors, they were able to redefine what freedom meant for their existential situation. For many African Americans, freedom is the absence of oppression and the ability to live out God's calling in one's life. The challenge of clearly defining freedom in African American Christianity happens when the individualistic expressions of the term get intertwined with a more social perspective.

Freedom is both an individual and a social endeavor for many African American Christians who understand their relationship with Jesus in personal terms but hope for transformation for the entire black community. This interplay between personal and social freedom ultimately gets translated into an interplay between personal and social salvation. Many slaves resonated with Christian messages advocating for freedom from sin and inward change. Yet, experiencing years of oppression in the United States also led them to interpret freedom, and ultimately salvation, through a social lens. The slaves believed God wanted them to change, but they also believed God wanted them to be free as a people. African American soteriology is intimately connected to freedom language as it pertains to the individual and the community.

Within the American context this interplay between the personal and the social is even more convoluted for African Americans because of the individualistic nature of the underlying American dream and what it has meant for blacks. Lincoln and Mamiya write:

> For whites freedom has bolstered the value of American individualism: to be free to pursue one's destiny without political or bureaucratic interference or restraint. But for African Americans freedom has always been communal in nature. In Africa the destiny of the individual was linked to that of the tribe or the community in an intensely interconnected security system. In America, black people have seldom been perceived or treated as individuals; they have usually been dealt with as "representatives" of their "race," an external projection.[5]

American Christianity focuses on individual freedom and ultimately individual salvation, but African Americans are often lumped together and not treated as real persons. For African Americans the denial of real personhood means that living out the American dream is not realistic. If the American dream is about individual achievement, then society has to see the individual as a real person. African Americans who chase the American dream always walk a tightrope between being called sellouts or perceived as assets to the black community. The interplay between personal and social freedom (salvation) becomes a negotiation to maintain communal ties while living out one's personal destiny.

In part, this is what DuBois names as "double consciousness."[6] Most African Americans are faced with their personal aspirations, which closely resemble the American dream and certain strands of conversion Christianity, over against the social aspirations of the community as a whole. I am reinterpreting DuBois's original meaning of double consciousness to illustrate the ongoing dilemma African Americans face as Christians in the United States and to provide some insight into why black soteriological perspectives focus on freedom.

African American soteriological perspectives have to negotiate the interplay between personal and social salvation, realizing the inherent challenge in this process because of the lived reality of blacks in America. Defining salvation as *personal* resonates with the conversion tradition that many African Americans experience and with the underlying reality of the American dream, but it also perpetuates many of the current systemic structures that originated in slavery. Defining salvation as *social* resonates with the communal heritage of Africa and maintains the responsibility of the individual to the community, but it also reinforces the invisibility of many African Americans, who only become real through the community spokesperson. The three schools of thought (liberationist, reconciliation, and survivalist) negotiate the interplay between personal and social salvation in their effort to construct a soteriology that speaks to this reality of African American lives and hopes.

School One: Liberation

James Cone is representative of those within the black liberation school. Black liberationists develop a model of soteriology connecting God's actions for the oppressed to salvation. Cone argues that liberation means no longer experiencing the "death-dealing political, economic, and social structures of society."[7] The focus of this black liberation model is the power dynamic underlying social structures and how power gets translated into Christianity. Therefore, black liberationists broaden their soteriological perspectives from discussions about developing a relationship with Jesus to deconstructing the social ills oppressing communities. Broadening soteriology in this way does not negate more traditional understandings of salvation, but it does rethink the meaning and practices connected to soteriology.

Black liberationists do not begin with the assumptions or theological doctrines that many Euro-American theologians use in developing their soteriological perspectives (for example, justification). They begin with the particularity of the black experience in the United States and develop a soteriology that addresses African American lives. Therefore, a black liberationist's understanding of soteriology, while sharing some of the same commitments as the Wesleyan approaches discussed in the last chapter, differs in three important ways: (1) it redefines eschatological hope, (2) the Exodus event is paradigmatic, and (3) Jesus' life is essential to the salvation process. In developing these themes this chapter will illustrate why a black liberationist's approach to soteriology deconstructs the power dynamic inherent in societal structures.

The emphasis for many black liberationists is the social aspect of salvation and not the personal. They attempt to correct the overemphasized individualistic expressions of salvation that many slaves experienced and address the structures of oppression that continue to bind African Americans. Cone writes this about personal expressions of salvation that push for an otherworldly hope:

> We come back to this question again: What about life after death? On the one hand, black theology believes that the emphasis on heaven in black churches was due primarily to white slave masters whose intention was to transfer slaves' loyalties from earthly reality to heavenly reality. In that way, masters could do what they willed about this world, knowing that their slaves were content with a better life in the next world. The considerable degree to which black slaves affirmed the worldview of masters was due to their inability to change life on earth. But the rise of black power and black theology brings with it a change in the focus of blacks.[8]

The change Cone touches on is a move toward deconstructing systemic structures oppressing African Americans in this world. Therefore,

Cone is always working with an eschatology that impinges upon the current structures of this world and not one that simply perceives this world as a prefatory state to the one to come. As a result, black liberationists are suspicious of models of soteriology that promote personal salvation in a way that neglects the systemic structures of oppression currently facing the oppressed. Such models remind many African Americans of the abuses heaped upon them by so-called Christian slave owners who had no interest in their earthly well-being. This means a black liberationist's soteriological model emphasizes an eschatology that makes salvation more than a personal future hope. Salvation is the deconstruction of structural oppression at all levels of society, or personal salvation loses its meaning.

Black liberationists are not suggesting that Christianity denies the reality of heaven or the hope of heaven. The reality of heaven has to be rethought from the perspective of the oppressed, not as an escape from this world, but as the ultimate hope of transforming this world. Cone points out:

> Black theology cannot reject the future reality of life after death—grounded in Christ's resurrection—simply because whites have distorted it for their own selfish purposes. That would be like the Black Art Movement rejecting art because white artists have misused it. What we need is redefinition in the light of the liberation of the black community.[9]

The point is that salvation has an otherworldly aspect for liberationists, but not one that compromises transformation in this world.

Black liberationists, however, emphasize that eschatology is perceived from the vantage point of the oppressed. The hope of the future is significant insofar as it relates to liberation in the present.[10] This counters the traditional message experienced during slavery by many African Americans who were taught about a better life over yonder. Black liberationists believe the reality of God's future is a present hope, and this means redefining eschatology in a way that never loses sight of this truth while maintaining the reality of heaven. Cone reminds African Americans this means that "those who die for freedom have not died in vain; they will see the kingdom of God."[11]

Harriet Tubman, who was the conductor of the Underground Railroad and a member of the AMEZ Church, embodied this eschatological approach. She made several runs between the South and the North, leading slaves to safety. The struggle for freedom was central to her ministry.

To separate her work as the conductor of the Underground Railroad from God's work of salvation negates the reality of God working in history. It is to this reality that black liberationists point as the paradigmatic hermeneutic of the Bible and model for soteriology.

Redefining soteriology to focus on God's action for the oppressed means the Exodus event becomes central to any discussion about salvation. Black liberationists maintain a dialectic between the Hebrew text and the meaning of Jesus' life, death, and resurrection. For example, the Exodus event is held in tension with the Jesus event. Many Euro-American scholars do not maintain such a tension in their soteriological perspectives. They tend to stick with more traditional ways of exploring soteriology that emphasize christological categories. Holding the Exodus story in tension with the Jesus event illustrates God's intent to physically liberate the oppressed. Cone comments: "In the Old Testament salvation is grounded in history and is identical with God's righteousness in delivering the oppressed from political bondage. Salvation is a historical event of rescue. It is God delivering the people from their enemies and bestowing upon Israel new possibilities within the historical context of her existence."[12]

Black liberationists use the Exodus event to exemplify God's work of salvation on behalf of the Israelites, and they argue that this is paradigmatic of God's salvific plan for all oppressed people. In fact, Jesus' work of salvation must be understood through an exodus paradigm because God's salvific work is about liberation and not about seeking paradise. Jesus was not part of the ruling class or the status quo, but was a poor Jew who described his ministry as good news to the oppressed. The Exodus event provides a frame for understanding God's work of liberation within history, both ancient Israel's history and as continued in the ministry, death, and resurrection of Jesus the Christ.

What makes the Exodus event so vital to understanding soteriology is that it includes a physical liberation component that traditional salvation models exclude. Cone reports, "By delivering this people from Egyptian bondage and inaugurating the covenant on the basis of that historical event, God is revealed as the God of the oppressed, involved in their history, liberating them from bondage."[13] God acts to liberate the Israelites from physical bondage at the hands of the Egyptians, which means salvation is more than just a spiritual expectation. Salvation for the oppressed includes no longer being in bondage or experiencing the structures of bondage.

The Hebrew text provides a lens for how we are to read the Jesus event as God's intent for all oppressed people in history. Reading Jesus' life, death, and resurrection through this lens moves God's work of salvation from the particularity of the Israelites to include all oppressed people.[14] African Americans know God will liberate them from their oppression and the structures of oppression because what God did for the Israelites is promised to all oppressed people in the Resurrection event. This promise represents a physical liberation from oppression and not just a spiritual one.

Obviously black liberationists believe God's salvific plan includes physical freedom from bondage for the oppressed. This is a sticking point, however, for many outside of this school of thought, including some Wesleyan scholars. Schubert Ogden considers this one of the central critiques against liberation theologies.[15] In part, Ogden suggests that liberation theologies confuse God's work of redemption with what he terms emancipation (liberation) because they are more interested in "action and justice," than in "belief and truth."[16] Ogden and others following his pattern of thought miss the point. They are interpreting redemption from the comfort of the oppressor and not as one of the oppressed. Cone writes:

> The task of theology, then, is to explicate the meaning of God's liberating activity so that those who labor under enslaving powers will see that the forces of liberation are the very activity of God. Christian theology is never just a rational study of the being of God. Rather it is a study of God's liberating activity in the world, God's activity in behalf of the oppressed.[17]

Certainly Ogden and Cone disagree on the task of theology and what this means for Christians. Ogden maintains that liberationists (he is all-inclusive in the way he uses the term) misunderstand the theological task because of an inadequate metaphysics about God.[18] The challenge for those supporting Ogden's position is the reality of African American Methodism and its starting point for understanding God.

Richard Allen did not walk out of Saint George's Methodist Episcopal Church because he was interested in debating the existence of God or figuring out the philosophical meaning of freedom. He walked out of Saint George's because he experienced oppression and sought actual freedom. Allen's exodus from Saint George's exemplifies the meaning of liberation for African American Methodists and the importance of starting with a contextual situation. The physical liberation of many African Americans was based upon their interpretation of God's action for the Israelites as a continuing reality in their lives. By keeping the Exodus event in tension with the Jesus event, liberationists create a different paradigm for interpreting and understanding soteriology.

Finally, black liberationists shift the way in which we should understand Christology by arguing for the inclusion of Jesus' life and ministry. Many soteriologies begin with Jesus' death and point to his resurrection as the key to God's work of salvation for humanity. Black liberationists agree that the death and resurrection of Jesus are central to understanding God's work of salvation, but they differ from many Euro-American Wesleyan soteriologies because they also emphasize Jesus' life. Cone contends:

> For without the historical Jesus, theology is left with a docetic Christ who is said to be human but is actually nothing but an idea-principle in a theological system. We cannot have a human Christ unless we have a historical Christ, that is, unless we know his history. That is why the writers of the four Gospels tell the good news in the form of the story of Jesus' life.[19]

For black liberationists the life of Jesus is central to the salvific work of God in history. Many Wesleyan scholars (that is, conversionists and gradualists in particular) make Jesus' life ancillary to the salvation process. This does not mean that these scholars believe Jesus' life is unimportant, but it does suggest that they believe Jesus' life should be compartmentalized because the social situation into which the incarnate One was born has little meaning for God's plan of salvation. The fact that Jesus was a Jew and a poor Jew gets lost or reinterpreted in some Wesleyan soteriologies. For example, the fact that Jesus was a poor Jew is not central to Maddox's interpretation of Wesleyan theology because his focus is more christological.

Certainly some Wesleyan scholars will argue that Wesley was committed to the poor, and this theme is prevalent in their theologies. The difference between the approach of many Wesleyan scholars and black liberationists on this issue of the poor is the role that power and context play in their analysis. Most Wesleyan scholars connect working with the poor (works of mercy) to what a Christian is called to do as a result of justification and the recovery of the moral image of God. For many Wesleyans, the fact that Jesus was a poor Jew oppressed by the Roman Empire plays little or no role in their analysis of context. The power dynamic inherent in Jesus' context gets downplayed and Jesus' spirituality moves to the forefront. Doing works of mercy is best understood as an appropriate response to God's love for humanity, with little thought given to systemic issues or context.

Contrast this with what black liberationists are suggesting and the difference is clear. Liberationists argue that salvation has to be interpreted through the lens of Jesus' social context. The fact that Jesus was incarnate as a poor Jew has significance for God's work of salvation in history. This shifts God's work of salvation from some abstract universal idea to the particularity of those who are oppressed in a given situation. Of course, many Euro-American theologians will argue all people are oppressed—we all can be oppressed spiritually. Such theologians miss the point liberationists are arguing and continue to frame soteriology in universal language that supports the status quo. The fact that Jesus did not come as part of the status quo means the particularity of Jesus' incarnation has significance for the oppressed, and this significance is more than just a spiritual freedom. The meaning of the Jesus of history is that God identifies with the oppressed, and salvation begins from this perspective and not from above.[20]

Jesus' identification with the oppressed has always had salvific importance in the Black Methodist Church. For example, the hymn that goes, "O freedom, O freedom . . . and before I'll be a slave, I'll be buried in my grave, and go home to my Lord and be free,"[21] when sung by many African Americans is not only a song pointing to some future hope but is also a song about the struggle to deconstruct the systemic structures oppressing blacks. The reinterpretation of hymns and songs to speak to African American social situations maintains the dialectic between the black social experience and Jesus' social context.[22] Thus, both the reality of oppression and God's working in history to destroy systemic evil and to bring about true salvation remain in this dialectical tension.

Black liberationists differ from many Wesleyan scholars because their soteriological approach starts with the African American experience in America and not with some universally constructed Christian experience. The different starting point between these scholars also translates into how they understand the command to love their neighbor. For Wesleyans, the command to love God and one's neighbor often means privileging the love of God. Because love of God is primary, they find it possible to separate it from their actions toward their neighbor. For example, slave owners could argue that they loved God while keeping African Americans in bondage because blacks were not defined as neighbors.

Black liberationists argue that loving one's neighbor means loving the oppressed. In fact, black liberationists start with the love of neighbor as the lens for our love of God. This shift defines "the least" as one's neighbor and changes what it means to love God. A slave owner could not claim to love God and still hold slaves using the logic of liberationists. By focusing on the oppressed, black liberationists redefine who our neighbor is and what salvation looks like for those not normally considered neighbors.

The fact that black liberationists are for the oppressed, however, does not exclude them from just-us behavior. Three critiques can be levied against a liberationist approach to soteriology. Two are internal critiques within the African American community and the third is an external critique Euro-American scholars often express.

First, one runs the risk of focusing too tightly on a particular form of oppression—race. For example, the early work of black theology deconstructs racial oppression but has little to say about gender oppression. Does this mean African American men are elect and African American women are not? Because of the work of individuals like Jacquelyn Grant, Delores Williams, and others, this is being corrected.

In the African American church and community at large a bias still exists toward maleness. The leadership in all of the African American Methodist denominations is overwhelmingly male. The AME Church did not elect its first female bishop until 2000, and the AMEZ Church just did it in 2008. My point is liberation continues to be framed from a male perspective rather than a gender-inclusive, communal one. This analogy holds true in the community at large when considering those individuals clamoring to be "leaders" of the African American community. A liberationist approach to soteriology is weakened in practice when the social fabric of the African American community continues to be biased toward maleness.

The second internal critique is a particular way in which individualistic strands of liberation are creating just-us issues within the African American community. Prosperity ministries focus on a strand of liberation (economic), but do so in a way that returns to individualism. Black liberationists argue that economic liberation is a part of the salvific process in order to change the circumstances of the oppressed. Prosperity ministries focus solely on individual economic gain and lose sight of the broader community. This ends up being another form of individualistic "me first" thinking that loses sight of a more holistic perception of salvation.

The challenge is how to articulate economic liberation in a way that does not suggest individualistic salvation. The Exodus event was about the entire community crossing the Red Sea and escaping from bondage. Harriet Tubman did not return only for her family but also conducted many slaves to safety. By focusing on individual economic gain and losing sight of the broader community, prosperity ministries transform liberation into another avenue to live out a personal Christianity at the expense of the community.

Another challenge under the rubric of individualistic strands of liberation for some black scholars is their de-emphasizing strands of personal salvation that have deep roots in expressions of African American soteriology. Personal salvation has always been central to the black church; and even though social freedom is also an issue, it has never negated strong conversion models. The Wesleyan conversion model actually resonates more than a black liberation model with some African Americans in congregations because of our history in the United States. Developing a stronger understanding of personal salvation that accurately reflects the theology of many African American congregants is something liberationists must do to reach the masses. A Pan-Methodist theology cannot ignore this part of African American Methodist heritage in moving forward toward a new soteriological model.

Third, a black liberationist approach to soteriology does not seemingly move toward reconciliation. This is a critique often stated by those in the Euro-American community. Specifically in Methodism, it suggests all of the denominations should reconcile once again. In the words of Rodney King, "Why can't we all just get along?" Certainly mistakes were made in the past and slavery was a horrible institution, but this is a new day and it is time to move forward with forgiveness. Those advocating for this position believe the evidence for living salvation is ultimately expressed in Christian unity here on earth as it will be in heaven.

A black liberationist approach to soteriology focuses on those things that have historically divided us as a community, which includes our Christian Methodist communities. Moving toward a Pan-Methodist theology means opening up dialogue with Euro-Americans or it continues to be a just-us theology. The real issue in moving forward is recognizing the tumultuous past relationship between the races. A Pan-Methodist theology has to negotiate the power dynamic inherent within the United

States that favors Euro-Americans while seeking real community with them. The theological importance of this challenge is it points toward true Christian community and what this looks like for Methodists.

School Two: Reconciliation

J. Deotis Roberts is representative of this school of thought within black theology. The individuals who advocate for reconciliation are not opposed to liberation; and they believe that, for Christians, liberation should ultimately lead to reconciliation. This school differs from a black liberationist's perspective because liberation is just one step in the process toward true Christian unity between blacks and whites. If Christianity is about all believers belonging to the body of Christ, then African Americans and Euro-Americans have to be reconciled within the body. This approach to salvation usually has the most affinity with Euro-American scholars because it seemingly values Christian unity by attempting to bring the races together and not perpetuating the divisions separating them.

Three themes shape reconciliationists' approach to soteriology, helping them construct a model that focuses on Christian unity: (1) liberation is a bridge between the races, (2) Jesus the Christ is liberator and reconciler, and (3) interracial cooperation is necessary. Reconciliationists argue that a soteriology that does not include reconciliation only half interprets God's intent for humanity. Roberts puts it in these words:

> It is only through vigorous protest—a crisis—precipitating interpretation of theology that the Christian faith, speaking and acting in and through the black church and the black community, may spark the revolution that may yet liberate all black people in this crisis-response society. But beyond liberation we chart the guidelines for a true Christian reconciliation. If we are warned that reconciliation is too futuristic for consideration at this time, we reply to our critics that in the nature of our faith we must always seek reconciliation. Christianity is rooted in the belief that "God was in Christ reconciling the world to Godself" (2 Cor. 5:19), and that reconciliation between God and humans can be effected only through reconciliation between persons.[23]

Liberation is important for African Americans as oppressed individuals within the American context, but reconciliation is also the ultimate measure of success for a Christian soteriology, and thus it is toward this end that both blacks and whites must strive.

How do you build a bridge between the races given the history of abuse suffered by African Americans in the United States? Reconciliationists develop a model that reinterprets the traditional soteriological categories of sin and forgiveness. Sin continues to be defined in terms of ego or self-centeredness, but these ideas for sin take on new meanings that focus on racism.[24] For example, sin is described as a form of bondage enslaving Euro-Americans because of their assumptions of superiority to African Americans.[25] Reconciliationists are not naive concerning the structural nature of racism. Reconciliationists agree with black liberationists that racism is structural and that personal salvation does not grant one a pass from this form of sin.

The two schools also agree that for the United States to truly become a community for all people, the sin of racism has to be eradicated.[26] The challenge, however, in eradicating racism is it is both personal and structural. At one level, racism functions between particular humans and requires transforming relationships between individuals. At another level, racism is systemic and requires the transformation of society itself. It is the transformation of society that is the most difficult to imagine. In part, it is difficult to imagine because figuring out forgiveness on a collective level continues to be a real challenge.[27]

This is one reason reconciliationists are careful to argue that forgiveness is contingent upon repentance.[28] This means true forgiveness requires a transformation by the oppressor in attitude and in actions. Forgiveness is also challenging for the oppressed because it means a willingness to offer it to the oppressor. Roberts summarizes the challenge facing both sides in the following manner:

> The problem confronting whites, even so-called Christians, in reference to blacks is that they cannot repent. Some whites are indifferent to the black person's plight; others assume no responsibility for these adverse conditions. By declaring "I am not a racist," they seek to free themselves of any ties with those of their race who have been and who are currently responsible for the misuse of White Power. Blacks, however, find forgiveness as almost impossible. What whites have done to blacks is so "demonic" that hate and revenge seem to be the only proper attitudes. It is not difficult to understand why Black Muslims refer to whites as "devils" and why religious Black Nationalists often seek to limit love and forgiveness to soul brothers and sisters. But it is sinful not

> to be able to forgive, just as it is sinful not to be able to repent. Both are unpardonable and are based upon a lack of sensitivity.[29]

For the possibility of reconciliation to occur in race relations, repentance and forgiveness are necessary steps. Reconciliationists affirm that both African Americans and Euro-Americans must step up to the plate and take responsibility for their role in the process. In this model, soteriology is about African Americans and Euro-Americans striving together with God's grace to resolve racism; it is not limited to the oppressed developing the right solution. It opens up possibilities for a soteriology where the oppressed and oppressor develop a model together, shaped by repentance and forgiveness.

Developing a soteriological model together that moves away from just-us thinking not only means creating a bridge, but also understanding the role of Jesus the Christ as both liberator and reconciler. Black liberationists emphasize that Jesus the Christ is ultimately about freedom from oppressive structures. Reconciliationists agree that Jesus the Christ is about freedom but believe Jesus is also about reconciliation. The particularity of who Jesus the Christ was as a poor Jew is important for African Americans, but the universality of Jesus the Christ moves African Americans toward reconciliation with the rest of humanity.[30] Liberation is not simply about freedom; it participates in reconciliation, which is the ultimate goal of Christianity.

As a liberator, Jesus the Christ enters into the African American situation and reinforces the personhood of those who are often invisible.[31] This affirms that every person is a child of God, without denying the sacredness of another. Freedom in this case is a freedom to live with the knowledge that one is not defined by others or by the systemic structures of society. Because of the way Jesus died and suffered, the Christ figure takes on the suffering of those who are experiencing oppression at the hands of another and works to liberate them from their situations. Jesus the Christ does not do this by destroying the oppressor but rather by affirming the significance of those oppressed.

Therefore, Jesus the Christ is able not only to liberate those oppressed; Jesus can reconcile them to their oppressor. This is accomplished because, like Jesus, the oppressed turn their suffering into something that opens up possibilities for reconciliation. Roberts writes:

> On the cross Christ gives himself to humankind. Black men and women, reconciled to God through the cross of Christ, but who through

> their suffering, their own cross-bearing, share the depth of his suffering, are purified, mellowed, and heightened in sensitivity and compassion. Thus healed and released in their own life, they may now become healers of others. The God, who through Christ reconciles the world to Godself, sends us forth to be agents of reconciliation. To such a witness in a broken world, blacks may not only be "called," but indeed "chosen."[32]

The language of "chosen" is important because it suggests that African Americans had to suffer in order for blacks and whites to be reconciled. Of course, Roberts is reinterpreting traditional christological language, which argues Jesus the Christ had to suffer so we can be saved. The point is that those oppressed are agents of reconciliation to their oppressors in a similar fashion as Jesus the Christ is to a sinful world. Although I applaud the goal of reconciliationists in trying to move toward Christian unity, the use of "chosen" to describe the role of African Americans in the reconciliation process is questionable. It creates the impression that African American enslavement was a part of God's plan for reconciliation and ultimately for salvation. This seemingly contradicts their point of Jesus the Christ valuing all persons as children of God, if some are used to reconcile others to God. More can be said about this issue and I will do so at the end of this section in my critique of this school of thought.

Because reconciliationists emphasize Christian unity, they place a high priority on communication between the races. For communication between the races to be effective, African Americans and Euro-Americans must treat one another as equals. Inherent in the process of communication is a certain amount of liberation because African Americans and Euro-Americans are practicing and living into reconciliation. Roberts recognizes that this form of communication does not come easily. He writes:

> A Black theology that takes reconciliation seriously must work at the task of intercommunication between blacks and whites under the assumption that for those who are open to truth, there may be communication from the inside out, but at the same time there may be communication from the outside in. In the latter sense, white Christians may be led to understand and work with blacks for liberation and reconciliation on an interracial basis.[33]

The critical component of Robert's suggestion is the idea of an interracial coalition. Roberts argues the term *interracial* "allows for two-way participation" and communication between the races.[34] In contrast, he dislikes the word *integration* because it assumes the same superior and inferior structure coming out of slavery that maintains Euro-American power.[35] An integration model means communication continues to be one-sided or from the top down (Euro-Americans to African Americans). An interracial model for communication means both sides participate equally in the process, allowing African Americans to work for and experience a certain level of liberation in the process.

Reconciliationists also dislike the idea of separatism favored by some within a stricter black liberationist camp. Separatism within the United States is not realistic since African Americans do not have their own state (land).[36] Reconciliationists perceive their position (interracial) as realistic because it negotiates the power dynamic of integration and avoids the impracticality of separatism. Soteriologically this means the oppressor cannot define salvation language, and it means salvation cannot hinge on a separatism that is defined in terms of the chosen few. Interracial cooperation means struggling together for a better eschatological future that changes the present circumstances of oppressed and oppressor.

A reconciliationist model more closely resembles the Wesleyan soteriological options than does the liberation model, when it comes to loving God and one's neighbor. The one difference is that reconciliationists emphasize racial repentance and forgiveness as the way to love God and neighbor. Both African Americans and Euro-Americans have a way to go to live out what it means to love God and their neighbor. The best way to accomplish loving God and neighbor in the context of the United States is an interracial approach that enables both races to strive together. For reconciliationists, God's love is about freedom—but it is not about a freedom that separates us from our neighbor. It is a freedom that liberates us to reconcile with our neighbor so that we are truly recovering the image of Christ—the author of reconciliation.

At first glance, critiquing a reconciliation model seems difficult given its affinity for bringing the races together; however, this model does have some inconsistencies. First, the focus of the model is racial, meaning it does not integrate other forms of oppression into its analysis. Gender and class are just a couple of the easy examples that womanist scholars continually point out are left out of many African American male liberationists'—and in this case also reconciliationists'—works. For the model to really speak to the whole African American community it needs to address more than just racial issues.

Second, a reconciliationist approach maintains the structural advantage of oppressors. Certainly this is not the intent of reconciliationists, and they argue against doing this very thing, but their model resonates with the current power dynamic. Cone comments:

> Whenever black people have entered into a mutual relation with white people, with rare exceptions, the relationship has always worked to the detriment of our struggle. From the abolitionist movement of the nineteenth century to the recent civil rights struggle of the 1950s and 60s, whites demonstrated that they cannot follow but must always lead. Thus there was a split between Frederick Douglass and William Garrison, Henry Garnet and Maria Chapman.[37]

The problem with a reconciliation model is it provides an avenue for Euro-Americans to set the agenda for African Americans within a black cultural context where whiteness defines power. The power dynamic has not changed; therefore, reconciliation and ultimately salvation are still defined by the oppressor. In moving toward a Pan-Methodist theology, this is a huge sticking point that must be addressed. How can Methodists of all races strive together without perpetuating systemic power structures?

Some Euro-Americans will react negatively to the claim that a reconciliation model necessitates maintaining white power. They will suggest that there are many examples of African Americans and Euro-Americans working together for better racial conditions. This argument misses the point of the critique to the extent that many Euro-Americans consciously and unconsciously perpetuate the structures of oppression, because whiteness equates to power. This does not mean all Euro-Americans are bad or are not becoming more conscious of their privileges, but it does mean as humans we often fail to understand how we benefit from structures that are an advantage to us. This is true within the African American church community where many black males perpetuate the structures benefiting them. Transforming the power dynamic in a situation of oppression is not easy, and reconciliation models often perpetuate these structures.

Third, redefining the language of "chosen" to mean African Americans were called to suffer is another form of maintaining the current power dynamic. The problem is that if God called African Americans to suffer, then the suggestion is that Euro-Americans were meant to be in power.

Certainly this is not the intent of reconciliationists, but the logic of their claim moves in this direction. Trying to equate African American suffering with what Jesus the Christ did for humanity is a dangerous proposition because it sets up models of salvation that place the onus on the oppressed. In fact, it sets up an expectation whereby the oppressed are valuable only to the extent that they exist for the oppressor. The strongest critique of this way of thinking comes from some in the womanist camp, which will be discussed in the next section of this chapter.

What should not be lost in the various challenges to a reconciliationist position is their point of striving together within the context of the United States. Liberation as a model only works to a certain extent because African Americans will always be the minority in this context. A Pan-Methodist soteriology has to negotiate this reality while still seeking to deconstruct the current power dynamics permeating American society. Although the intentions of reconciliationists are good, their methodology is inadequate.

School Three: Survivalist

Delores Williams, a womanist scholar, is representative of the survivalist school of thought. Williams develops a soteriological model that shifts traditional Christian beliefs in some significant ways, especially when it comes to the importance of the cross for salvific purposes. Williams' soteriology focuses on African American women and their struggle for survival in the United States. Survivalists differ from black liberationists because they do not interpret God as always seeking the liberation of the oppressed. In fact, they argue at times that the best we can hope for is to survive the systemic ills oppressing us.

Williams comments on discovering an alternative to the African American male liberation model:

> I made a startling discovery. I discovered that even though black liberation theologians used biblical paradigms supporting an androcentric bias in their theological statements, the African American community had used the Bible quite differently. For over a hundred years, the community had appropriated the Bible in such a way that black women's experience figured just as eminently as black men's in the community's memory, in its self-understanding and in its understanding of God's relation to its life.[38]

Survivalists are interested in giving voice to African American women and their understanding of freedom within the black community. A survivalist's perspective challenges the idea that freedom is synonymous with liberation, especially the liberation of African American women.

Although it is impossible to develop a detailed outline of a survivalist soteriology in this limited space, there are three interconnecting themes that differentiate a survivalist perspective from that of a black liberationist. First, survivalists offer an alternative paradigm to the Exodus motif that many black liberation scholars use. Survivalists begin with the Hagar stories and the importance of these stories for African American women. A survivalist's perspective reads the stories not from Abraham and Sarah's position, but from the position of Hagar, their slave.[39]

The reality of Hagar's relationship with Abraham, Sarah, and even God are constitutive for understanding African American female relationships with oppressors in the United States. In the Genesis stories Hagar is forced into motherhood, forced to return to her oppressor, forced into surrogacy roles, and eventually sent into the wilderness with almost no provisions for survival.[40] Survivalists believe these themes continue to impinge upon the lives of many African American women living in the United States. Williams writes:

> The African American community has taken Hagar's story unto itself. Hagar has "spoken" to generation after generation of black women because her story has been validated as true by suffering black people. She and Ishmael together, as family, model many black American families in which a lone woman/mother struggles to hold the family together in spite of the poverty to which ruling class economics consign it. Hagar, like many black women, goes into the wide world to make a living for herself and her child, with only God by her side.[41]

The Hagar stories offer an alternative understanding of soteriology that differs from the Exodus paradigm used by many African American male liberation scholars. The Exodus paradigm points toward freedom for all of God's elect people. A survivalist approach points out the problems with election, namely with who experiences freedom in the community. The Bible is replete with stories and examples of non-Hebrew individuals not experiencing liberation and the danger of making invisible those who are not considered elect.[42] Hagar is often invisible in the Genesis stories because many Christians interpret the story from the perspective of the oppressor (Abraham and Sarah). Interpreting Hagar's story and other stories from the perspective of those who the Israelites (non-Hebrews) enslaved paints a different picture for the meaning of freedom in relation to the Israelite community. Survivalists seek a soteriological approach that addresses the reality of those made invisible because of their status in the community.

Another soteriological difference survivalists perceive between their approach and that of black liberationists is that a black liberation model is more static. Focusing on the Exodus limits the meaning of liberation to coming out of slavery. Williams writes:

> I suggest that African American theologians should make it clear to the community that this black way of identifying with God solely through the exodus of the Hebrews and Jesus' reported words in Luke belongs to the black historical period of American slavery. Apparently this was the time when God's liberation of the Israelites or the exodus was the subject and "predicate" of the biblical ideas undergirding African American Christian theology. Such is not the case today.[43]

Williams makes a good point in terms of the Exodus motif and its emphasis on coming out of slavery; however, I disagree with her inclusion of Jesus' words in Luke 4 (she references Luke 4 right above the part I quoted). She limits the meaning of *oppressed* in a way that Jesus did not. In fact, Jesus' words in Luke 4 help her argument because Jesus works to make women in Jewish society visible in his ministry.

A second soteriological theme important for survivalists is the wilderness experience. The wilderness was both a freeing space and a hostile environment in African American culture.[44] Before emancipation it was a freeing space, because African American women and men often encountered God in the wilderness.[45] The wilderness was a space where slaves could go physically and meditate on God.[46] The isolation of the wilderness offered slaves protection from their oppressors, enabling them to come face-to-face with God.[47] The wilderness was also a space where runaway slaves found shelter from their oppressors and were able to find food or plants needed for healing.[48] Prior to emancipation (that is, the early 1800s) the wilderness was a space where slaves could journey and experience different levels of transformation, from religious to physical healing.[49]

After emancipation the wilderness takes on a different connotation that is more hostile. The wilderness represents the cold world where African American women must journey to make a "living for their families."[50] The economic reality of having to provide for a family, given the structural oppression existing in the United States, altered the view of wilderness for many African Americans. Two postemancipation views of the wilderness frame African American thinking and make a strong connection to the Hagar narratives.[51] The wilderness is a freeing space where one can encounter God, but it is also a hostile place where stark economic realities hit home. The Hagar narratives illumine this reality in the way she is proactive in naming God but also needs assistance to survive out in the wilderness with no provisions.

Williams summarizes the connection between Hagar and African American women in this way:

> The similarities between these women's plight and faith and Hagar's is striking. Like Lou Emma Allen, Hagar must have been afraid in the wilderness, pregnant and alone. Like Susie Morgan, Hagar had a word with God, and radical obedience was her response to God's will. Like Ethel Gray, Hagar suffered indignities and abuse from those who had more power than she did, but she defied them by resisting their authority over her movements. These Mississippi women and Hagar had their wilderness experience of courage, fear, aloneness, meeting God and obeying God's will for transformations in their lives. Finally, all the women and Hagar could testify, "Me and God stood up."[52]

Soteriologically, the wilderness is a space where experiencing God is possible even in the midst of structural oppression working to make one invisible. The wilderness is a space where survival is possible because the oppressor has no control over that space. It allows those made invisible by the structures of the culture to survive and be transformed in such a way that they live to fight another day. This transformation includes the mind, body, and spirit of the individual, and possibly the community. In short, a black liberation model addresses the exodus from slavery, but it is a survivalist's approach that sustains the African American community as they wander through the wilderness seeking God's guidance while trying to survive in a hostile world.

The third theme important for a survivalist's model is Jesus' ministry. The issue for survivalists is how humanity is saved. Is humanity saved by the sacrificial death of Jesus the Christ, or as survivalists posit, is humanity saved by Jesus' life of resistance? Survivalists reject models of salvation that portray Jesus as a sacrificial lamb. The problem with these models is that they perpetuate for African American women surrogacy roles that society places on them. Williams argues, "To respond meaningfully to black women's historic experience of surrogacy oppression, the womanist theologian must show that redemption of humans can have nothing to do with any kind of surrogate or substitute role Jesus was reputed to have played in a bloody act that supposedly gained victory over sin and/or evil."[53]

Survivalists shift the importance of Jesus' death on the cross from one of surrogacy to a ministerial vision for how humanity is to resist oppression.[54] This ministerial vision focuses on creating right relations among the mind, body, and spirit.[55] Resisting oppression does not guarantee liberation, and it may mean doing all an individual or a community can do in order to survive. Resisting oppression does, however, mean inviting all humans to participate in the work of creating right relations that move us individually and as a community toward wholeness. This movement toward wholeness is not dependent on Jesus becoming a sacrifice for humanity but rather focuses on how Jesus' life and ministry illustrate the capacity to resist and survive structural oppression.

A survivalist approach to soteriology deconstructs traditional redemption models that depend on Jesus as a surrogate for humanity. The aim is to develop a salvific model that frees African American women from worshiping surrogacy. African American women have historically been placed in various forms of surrogacy within the United States, and traditional models of redemption reinforce these roles. The question is, *Does a survivalist's redemptive model fully represent the majority of African American women in the pews?* Because of the survivalists' emphasis on Jesus' ministerial vision, loving God and one's neighbor requires participating in creating right relations. The language of right relations is familiar; it is rhetoric many Wesleyan scholars use in their theologies. Survivalists, however, are suggesting something different that interprets loving God and neighbor, not from the perspective of the cross but from that of the hope inherent in Jesus' earthly ministry. This means God's love for humanity is not one of reconciling us to God through the sacrifice of Jesus the Christ. God's love for humanity is grounded in developing and living out relationships that empower all individuals and communities to flourish.[56]

A survivalist approach to human flourishing is different because surrogacy does not undergird this model. Loving God and one's neighbor does not require a form of sacrificing that places individuals in powerless positions where others oppress them. Human flourishing means that loving God and one's neighbor creates an arena where the other is made visible and is valued as a whole person. Certainly the other soteriologies discussed have this same hope, but survivalists argue that their approaches depend on traditional redemptive models of surrogacy. A survivalist approach maintains the hope for human flourishing through loving God and one's neighbor, but rejects any forms of surrogacy that undergird such flourishing.

A survivalist soteriological model pushes all of the other approaches discussed because it rejects traditional redemptive paradigms. The logic behind rejecting traditional salvific paradigms for African American women makes sense given the history of surrogacy and the roles they are and were forced to play in the United States. A critique does not challenge the logic of rejecting the traditional models of redemption but focuses on the lack of bridge-building for the community survivalists represent.

Womanist theology developed to give voice to African American women who were made invisible by other theologies, including black liberation theology. The strength of the survivalist model is it deconstructs other theological approaches by illustrating how they perpetuate surrogacy roles for African American women. The challenge, however, for Williams's interpretation of this model pertaining to soteriology, is it starts on one side of a huge canyon and jumps to the other side without building a bridge to make the journey for those it represents. In other words, many African American women probably agree with the analysis on surrogacy and the roles black women have been forced to play in the United States. The problem is some of these same women are very committed to the more traditional redemptive models because they perceive them as healing.

Although a survivalist model is not incongruent with African American women's experience, some African American women need a stronger bridge to make it to the other side of the canyon, where this approach seeks to lead them. Williams writes at one point:

> Perhaps not many people today can believe that evil and sin were overcome by Jesus' death on the cross; that is, that Jesus took human sin upon himself and therefore saved humankind. Rather, it seems more intelligent and more scriptural to understand that redemption had to do with God, through Jesus, giving humankind new vision to see the resources for positive, abundant, relational life. Redemption had to do with God, through the *ministerial* vision, giving humankind the ethical

> thought and practice upon which to build positive, productive quality of life.[57]

This statement undermines the strength of a survivalist's position because it suggests that intelligent people will no longer interpret redemption in a traditional manner. Even if this is not the intent of the statement, and Williams is trying to illustrate the positive side of God's salvific work through Jesus, the statement is open to that interpretation. Unfortunately, it creates a false dichotomy. If her point is to encourage African American women to rethink suffering based upon their situations, then more clarity on how to do this and changing her use of language may be appropriate.

My intent is not to perpetuate black androcentrism but rather to highlight a way in which a survivalist's model can better connect with those it represents. A survivalist's perspective was and is a needed corrective to a black liberation model. If we are going to make a difference in the pews, then our approaches have to build bridges for those in congregations to come with us, or for us to journey with them.

Just-us: Contextualizing Freedom

The importance of freedom has been discussed throughout this chapter as it relates to the different soteriological positions of black liberationists, reconciliationists, and survivalists. One of the strengths of the various schools discussed is their strong contextual emphasis for Methodism within the United States. A challenge, however, for black liberationists and survivalists is the cognitive dissonance between the biblical paradigms they are using and the ultimate logic of those paradigms in the context of the United States. The biblical paradigms both schools are using move toward complete physical separation from the oppressor. In the Exodus event the Israelites leave Egypt in search of their own promised land, and in the Hagar narrative she is kicked out of the household and forced to make it on her own in the desert. A mass African American exodus from the United States is not likely at this point, and although it is possible to create wilderness experiences for a while, most African Americans are in physical contact with Euro-Americans daily. In the United States a complete physical separation is not possible.

Black liberationists and survivalists are absolutely on target in arguing that the shift from slavery to nonslavery is a physical change. Black liberationists are correct that Richard Allen's leaving Saint George's

Methodist Episcopal Church was an exodus event that resulted in physical freedom. Survivalists are right in arguing that the wilderness at one time was both a place of freedom and a hostile place where African American women went to make a way out of no way. The problem, however, is the biblical models used by both schools hinge on a complete physical separation from the oppressor. Ultimately, the biblical models used by both schools suggest that true freedom is only possible when creating your own nation-state separate from your oppressor.

The Exodus event is central to Israelite history because it represents the entire nation leaving Egypt and becoming a new nation. The Israelites did not stay in Egypt and become a new nation; they left the structures of oppression. Similarly, Hagar's wilderness experience is an effort to separate herself from her oppressor. In the first Genesis account she is sent back to her oppressor and is oppressed again. In the second Genesis account she is kicked out of the family, but this action sets in motion her physical separation and freedom from her oppressor and the beginning of another nation. In both instances freedom means a complete physical separation from the structures of oppression.

The challenge of thinking about freedom in this manner is twofold. First, African Americans are unlikely to have a mass exodus from the United States to start their own nation. In fact, many African Americans rejected the American Society for Colonizing the Free People of Color movement and opted instead to struggle in the United States. This means the logic of the biblical paradigms in terms of complete separation from the oppressor is not possible. Second, the measurement for success in the biblical models is not learning to live in harmony, but creating your own power entity. Hagar's ancestors become a nation opposed to the Israelites. The Israelites quickly forget what it means to be oppressed when they start oppressing others in their quest for nationhood.

The just-us issues raised in the biblical paradigms that black liberationists and survivalists use can be interpreted as promoting that the only way to achieve justice is away from one's oppressor. The reality is the oppressed often leave and reenact the oppression they experienced. If justice is the goal, then learning to live together physically has to be a part of the puzzle. Certainly black liberationists and survivalists provide an epistemological way for African Americans to make it in the United States, and this is no small task. Both models, however, leave open the issue of redefining freedom in a manner that moves away from a cognitive dissonance that short-circuits new soteriological possibilities in the United States.

Some Wesleyans and even African Americans are probably pondering, *Why not just focus on a reconciliationist model?* If the issue is in part a power struggle, then why not simply focus on reconciliation and all parties coming together for a new future? In the United States it is tricky to use the term *reconciliation* about relationships between those with power and those without. Those with power like reconciliation rhetoric because they believe it maintains the status quo. They do not perceive reconciliation to mean transforming the status quo in favor of the oppressed. It is too early to think in terms of reconciliation if the goal is truly creating a new heaven and earth. Chapter 6 suggests an alternative to reconciliation called "engaging friendship" that is more appropriate for a Pan-Methodist soteriological model. The point is not to give up on the ideal of reconciliation, but to start with an alternative soteriology that is Pan-Methodist and not solely black liberationist, survivalist, or Wesleyan.

A Pan-Methodist soteriology struggles with the idea of freedom from the perspective of what this can look like when one stays in the oppressor's land. In other words, the biblical ideal of leaving physically and starting a new nation is not an option. A Pan-Methodist soteriology recognizes this limitation and seeks to develop a model that maintains the commitments of black liberationists and survivalists, and builds power structures in such a way that all individuals and communities are made visible so that all humans can flourish. Maintaining these commitments while attempting to fully engage Wesleyan thinking is no easy task, but this is the challenge of Pan-Methodism.

CHAPTER 5

MOVING TOWARD A PAN-METHODIST SOTERIOLOGY

Moving toward a Pan-Methodist soteriology will not resolve many of the ongoing problems within Methodism or various theological debates. For example, the challenge that African American and Wesleyan scholars currently face in trying to integrate personal and communal understandings of salvation will not be fully resolved by a Pan-Methodist approach. The unique development of Methodism in the United States, however, may provide clues to rethinking some just-us issues as they pertain to race, gender, and class. The Jena Six case is an example of the ongoing struggle between races in America and provides a lens for us to discuss the complexity of just-us.

The Jena Six case really caught the national attention of the news media in the fall of 2007. In Jena, Louisiana, six African American males are on trial for the beating of a Euro-American classmate. The issues relating to the beating have deep roots going back to some African American students wanting to congregate around a tree that had become for whites only. The result of their breaking this invisible barrier was that a noose was found hanging from the tree. The obvious inference was that the noose was a symbol for breaking the unwritten code of racial propriety. The situation in Jena is controversial because it highlights many of the ongoing problems in American culture; it is a case with soteriological ramifications.

This chapter will not analyze the case in detail, but by using it we can highlight an interesting theme related to moving toward a Pan-Methodist soteriology, namely how deep the roots of just-us still run in the American context. The idea that America has somehow moved beyond racial problems and, by implication, beyond gender and class issues, is a false claim. Already inbred in youth in Jena, Louisiana, and all over America, is an assumption that whiteness is superior to color. By analogy, I think similar assumptions can be made about gender, class, and other disenfranchising categories.

Issues like race, class, and gender that separate us in America are not simply cultural challenges but are also theological challenges that deeply influence our understanding of God and culture. The way we address the various systemic issues in America tends to move in one of three directions. We attempt to "fix" situations like the Jena Six case by sweeping them under the rug (completely ignoring them). Another strategy is distancing one's behavior from that which is being scrutinized at the time. And at times we attack an institution (for example, the judicial system) in hopes that this will solve all of the complex problems resulting from a particular situation.

In the Jena Six case, all three solutions were and are being attempted. The town initially tried to sweep the case under the rug by cutting down the tree that started the controversy. Cutting down the tree was symbolic of the town moving on and no longer having racial difficulties. Another strategy the town employed when media coverage increased involved some individuals saying that they personally were not racist and the prosecutor was just doing his job. Their point was racism may exist, but they personally did not adhere to racist ideals. Finally, others outside of Jena perceived this as an opportunity to create a stage for their forums. Protesting the injustices in Jena by pointing to the systemic inconsistencies in the judicial system is admirable, but the problem is when Jena becomes second-page news and the next story hits, who will be there helping the boys? I am guessing that many of you probably have not recently thought about or read anything related to the Jena Six case until I mentioned it in this chapter. Protesting against an institution only when it is convenient, without a concerted effort for lasting change, is another form of sweeping it under the rug.

The problem illumined by the Jena Six case is the same challenge we face within Methodism. Because the roots of just-us are so deep within Methodism, attempts are made to just sweep differences under the rug. For instance, African American and Euro-American Methodists often gloss over the denominational splits slavery caused and focus on a goal of Christianity on which all can agree—heaven. Certainly, this is an oversimplification and unfair to those who really want to move forward toward a common soteriological goal. The problem is the goal assumes a degree of equality in the way all parties are journeying toward the goal.

Class, gender, and racial differences are not perceived as pertinent to how the goal is viewed or attained.

Some Methodists agree that just sweeping it under the rug is inappropriate and what is needed is personal transformation that comes from individuals truly becoming disciples of Christ. The suggestion is that transforming individuals will eventually lead to the transformation of society and the church. Two problems often occur. First, some individuals believe that because they are able to succeed and prosper, all people should be able to do the same. These individuals are well intentioned but do not recognize that race, gender, and class play a role in their success. The idea of changing individuals to transform society is not completely false, but it ignores the systemic nature of just-us issues. Second, individuals are a part of systems, and systems can thwart the best intents. Asbury opposed slavery but compromised his antislavery stance in some instances in an effort to maintain solidarity in the church. This does not mean Asbury never experienced personal transformation, but it does point toward the challenge of living in systemic environments.

There are Methodists who suggest the only way to make society more just is for structural changes to occur. Changing the very structures of society will put all people on an even playing field and minimize the impact of race, gender, and class. The problem is structures are biased toward those who have the power, and most changes end up reflecting the interest of a particular group. Many African American males did not deconstruct gender and class oppression and perpetuated this form of oppression in black Methodist churches. Although many African American males were interested in changing racial oppression, they did not have the same interest in changing gender and class oppression. The truth is many African American males benefited from gender and class oppression.

This is why issues like the Jena Six case are complicated and the theological approaches we suggest often fall short. Categories like race, gender, and class are so structural that soteriologies grounded in personal transformation are inadequate to fully address these issues. Yet soteriologies aimed at structural transformation are also inadequate to fully address these issues if they assume that systems can be changed apart from the people who exist in them. I am still convinced, however, that a soteriological approach that understands the dynamic of American culture can move us toward a different vision that negotiates these realities. The truth is no soteriological approach can resolve all the issues discussed above completely, but something different is needed for American Methodism to be relevant to its context.

Therefore, the goal in this chapter is to construct a soteriology that is Pan-Methodist and not just Wesleyan or just grounded in African American theological approaches. This is a formidable challenge given the diversity of soteriological perspectives in Methodism. A construction of a Pan-Methodist approach will not integrate all of the different soteriological themes into one great reconciling ideal. It is my intent to develop a soteriological approach that is contextual to American Methodism but universal in its possible applications. Such an approach requires a shift from current African American and Wesleyan soteriological approaches that moves us toward an embodied soteriology. Certainly, important themes from Wesleyan and African American approaches will inform a Pan-Methodist soteriology, but they will do so in a way that moves us toward a different soteriological vision.

Embodied Soteriology

Other theologians have suggested embodied approaches to theology. Feminist theologians are still in the forefront of embodied theological perspectives, but others from various camps are joining them. In arguing for an embodied soteriology for Pan-Methodism, this approach does not focus on gender but seeks instead to connect three themes: (1) incarnation, (2) moving toward true humanity, and (3) the wounds of Jesus. The incarnation is both helpful and challenging. The incarnation is helpful because it concretizes God becoming flesh. At the same time, the incarnation is a challenge because God becomes flesh as a Jewish male. The dialectic between these two realities has a lot to do with how we understand our bodies.

For Christians, and especially those within the Wesleyan tradition, moving toward true humanity is important. The goal is to become truly human in the same way that Jesus was fully human on Earth. The fact that Jesus still has the wounds on his hands and in his side after the Resurrection points to the pain of transformation and the reality of ongoing embodiment. As Christians, we cannot ignore that Jesus returns in bodily form, but does so without erasing the evidence of the Crucifixion. These three themes form the basis for an embodied soteriology.

Incarnation

The power of Christianity is the fact that God comes in human form. This means Christianity is an incarnational faith that takes the body seriously. Most Christians agree with and support the claim of incarnation. However, it is more controversial to claim, as does feminist theologian Sallie McFague, "The story of Jesus suggests that the shape of God's body includes all, especially the needy and outcast."[1] Many Christians at first glance will not find the last sentence controversial and may even develop their own metaphors of the body of Christ to illustrate how God's body does include everyone. The problem is incarnation usually becomes synonymous with a systemic privilege like race, gender, or class. For example, the embodiment of Jesus the Christ is a metaphor for the church, argues McFague, as long as the head most closely resembles that of a Euro-American male.[2] The tendency for most of us is to translate incarnation to mean Jesus takes on my form.

This is only a part of the challenge of incarnation as it pertains to just-us issues. Those in power interpret the incarnation to their advantage because it maintains the status quo. Those excluded from power react to those in power and redefine the incarnation of Jesus from their perspective. The problem is their redefinition usually ends up recapitulating the same oppressive practices toward someone else. In his essay, "Repetition, or the Theological Failures of Modern Dignity Discourse: The Case of Frederick Douglass's 1845 *Narrative*," J. Kameron Carter illustrates this point. Carter argues that Douglass uses his autobiography to redefine human dignity for African Americans but ends up recreating a similar structure of indignity for African American women.[3]

Although incarnation is at the heart of the Christian message, and most Christians will agree all are included in the body of Christ, the shape or form of the body is interpreted differently depending on who is in power. The real issue is how to interpret or discuss the incarnation in a way that deconstructs power without simply replacing it with a new form of systemic oppression. For those in power this means dealing with static assumptions. John Cobb argues that, in thinking about race in the United States, this means asking a different question than normal. Cobb suggests: "In any case, the dominant white approach, even the liberal one, locates the problem of race at the wrong place. Prior to the question about how the 'black race" can attain an equal place in American society is the question: What is meant by American society? For most whites, American society is white American society."[4]

By altering the question, we change our assumptions and possibly nuance our answers. The question of how African Americans can attain an equal place in American society assumes maintaining the status quo and Euro-American power. Shifting the question to, *What is meant by American society?* deconstructs static claims of power and opens up the possibility of not repeating systemic power plays.

The soteriological challenge for Methodists is developing an incarnational perspective that deconstructs static assumptions and opens up the possibility for not repeating systemic power plays. Karen Baker-Fletcher suggests we can best do this by differentiating between the "conquering Christ of Western imperialism" and the Jesus experienced by Sojourner Truth.[5]

The former is idolatrous because it is not the Jesus of the Gospels. The latter is consistent with the Jesus in the Gospels. Baker-Fletcher deconstructs notions of incarnation that equate Jesus the Christ with worldly empires, but she also moves toward a vision of incarnation challenging us to struggle against systemic oppression.

A Pan-Methodist approach supports incarnational thinking that is contextual, but not incarnational thinking that is idolatrous. The line between contextualizing the gospel and idolatry is very ambiguous. Pan-Methodists can negotiate this line by asking, *To what is God calling us?* Another way to frame this question is to ask, *What does prevenient grace mean for Pan-Methodists?* The answer is twofold. It means being in relationship with the Triune God. It also means systemic evil is limited.

God invites us to be in relationship with the Trinity. God does not leave humanity without any capacity of entering into relationship with the Trinity. Wesleyan theologian Kenneth J. Collins interprets prevenient grace in the following manner: "This grace is 'free for all,' not limited to the accidents of geography or culture, and it is 'free in all to whom it is given,' not dependent on any human power and merit. It is inclusive not exclusive; freely given not merited."[6] This invitation can be resisted. God does not force us to enter into a transforming relationship with the Trinity.

Prevenient grace accomplishes more than just enabling a relationship with the Triune God; it prevents evil from overcoming good.[7] Baker-Fletcher proposes, "Divine preventing grace in the providence/nurture of God keeps evil from overcoming the freedom to consciously experience and participate in divine love."[8] A belief in prevenient grace means even though humans are fallen and have free will, humanity cannot completely pervert God's creation. God is always working to call humanity to participate in God's plan of salvation.

An incarnational approach simultaneously moves us toward fleshing out the gospel and prevents us from forming the gospel in our bodily shape. This requires really seeing the body of the other and not simply spiritualizing the other, in the same way that Mamie Till-Mobley forced the country to see the body of her son when she left his casket open.[9] The country could not close its eyes to the evil that was perpetrated against Emmett Till.[10] God's word takes shape in particular contexts and calls us into a relationship that opens our eyes to evil in new ways.

Thinking about the incarnation from this perspective recognizes the priority of God's actions for humanity. Salvation is not a human effort, but is a divine process that invites human participation. When we claim to be Christian, and particularly Pan-Methodist, this means we believe God is calling us to participate in the divine process of salvation, which will open our eyes to systemic evils in ways we never imagined. We can no longer be comfortable with oppressive constructs of race, gender, and class because our eyes are open to really seeing the flesh of the other.

Linking how we think about prevenient grace to the incarnation accomplishes two things. First, prevenient grace points us toward the incarnation, or the gospel taking bodily form in a particular context. The bodily form the gospel takes is not limited to white Americans or black Americans but comes in many forms, including some we may not comprehend. Jacquelyn Grant points out:

> Even though Black women have been able to transcend some of the oppressive tendencies of White male (and Black male) articulated theologies, careful study reveals that some traditional symbols are inadequate for us today. The Christ understood as the stranger, the outcast, the hungry, the weak, the poor, makes the traditional male Christ (Black and White) less significant.[11]

God calls us to see the gospel in many bodily forms and not simply to recapitulate our own bodies. This is a major shift from the expectations the culture places upon us, but it is exactly the shift we are called to embody as Christians.

Second, the incarnation reminds us of the importance of prevenient grace. When Christians see the gospel fleshed out before their eyes, it is a reminder that God is calling them to participate in the divine plan of salvation. If it were not for God supernaturally restoring some measure of free will to humanity, then the significance of the incarnation could be redefined in nonsoteriological ways. By this I mean incarnational thinking makes visible what God calls us to do and be through God's prevenient grace. Jesus embodied for us a life dedicated to struggling against imperialism and other forms of oppression while maintaining a personal relationship with the first person of the Trinity. God not only calls us to see systemic evil in new ways while being in relationship with the Triune God, but God also comes into human form and embodies what it means to disclose systemic oppression and to struggle against it.

The story of the Jena Six helps illustrate both the linkage and importance of prevenient grace to incarnational thinking. The hanging of the noose on the tree was an opportunity for the community to confront systemic evil head-on. Everyone initially lost this opportunity to answer the call to participate in God's plan of salvation. Euro-Americans perpetuated privileging whiteness and denying people of color any fleshly existence. African Americans responded by trying to negate whiteness in the wrong manner. In both instances, a better understanding of the connection between prevenient grace and incarnational thinking could have changed the situation. An embodied soteriological approach means we are continuously called upon to answer God's calling in particular contexts with the knowledge that we must truly see the other in bodily form and not just as a shadow of ourselves.

True Humanity

If incarnational thinking is linked to prevenient grace, then the idea of what it means to be truly human is linked to justification. Admittedly, linking true humanity to justification is problematic on many fronts, one of which is Jesus the Christ being called to sacrifice for all of humanity and the implication this has for many disenfranchised individuals. Although this study does not address in detail sacrifice and many of the other issues related to linking justification to true humanity, it is clear that an embodied approach offers a perspective for linking these ideas that alters some traditional ways of thinking soteriologically.

For Pan-Methodists, linking true humanity and justification creates a space for understanding Jesus' life as central to the cross. This linkage between Jesus and the cross is important because it gives us a narrative for understanding the way some in the culture seek to silence the embodiment of justice. At the same time, it can challenge understandings of justification that seemingly justify placing women and other disenfranchised people in surrogate roles by not allowing those in power to determine the ultimate meaning of the cross—and by inference, humanity. One of the problems with defining what we mean by "human" is that humanity gets interpreted through a culturally specific lens and often ends up resembling those in power. Cobb describes the challenge in this manner:

> Unfortunately, history is replete with instances in which one identity subordinates others and thus rigidifies the we/they distinction. Also, loyalty to one community often precludes loyalty to more inclusive ones. A community that claims this exclusive loyalty can enter into temporary alliances with others to gain specific ends, but it cannot become part of a community of communities. The relation among such communities can only be competitive. The well-being of one requires losses by the others.[12]

To go even further, although Cobb does not make this point, this is true even when we are struggling not to disenfranchise others but do so by virtue of our positions in society. The reality is, the way we live out our existence as humans often creates chasms that thwart our attempts at coming together.

Therefore, one of the challenges when we think about justification from the perspective of the rigid distinctions created in American culture is that traditional understandings of this doctrine of salvation only intensify the chasms instead of bringing us closer together. For example, from such a perspective it may seem that women cannot properly preach or pastor because Jesus was a male. The argument is that this is not denying the humanity of women; but it can be and has been interpreted that there are different roles men and women play in bringing the reign of God into fruition. The implication is the only way to be fully justified is to be male; women are automatically disqualified.

Given the concerns expressed by some womanists or feminists and liberationists concerning the doctrine of justification, how do we hold on to the importance of Jesus the Christ's salvific work for us? An embodied approach starts with the assumption that Jesus' life must be perceived as a lens into the struggle for justice for individuals and communities. If we start with this assumption, then to be truly human means embodying the same struggle as Jesus the Christ. It also means understanding, as Jesus did, that many in the culture will attempt to silence "by any means necessary" the presence of God. Linking true humanity to justification in this manner both broadens and maintains some traditional understandings of the doctrine of justification. It broadens some traditional understandings of justification because Jesus' death cannot be construed strictly in personal language. It retains, however, Jesus the Christ's death and resurrection as the way to salvation.

For Pan-Methodists this means rethinking cultural assumptions about humanity through a liberation or survivalist lens, but with an understanding that the Easter event is salvific for humanity. James Cone develops this idea further from a liberationist perspective when he claims:

> Jesus Christ, therefore, in his humanity and divinity, is the point of departure for a black theologian's analysis of the meaning of liberation. There is no liberation independent of Jesus' past, present and future coming. He is the ground of our present freedom to struggle and the source of our hope that the vision disclosed in our historical fight against oppression will be fully realized in God's future. In this sense, liberation is not a human possession but a divine gift of freedom to those who struggle in faith against violence and oppression.[13]

Cone suggests two key statements in the above paragraph that are helpful in moving toward a Pan-Methodist soteriology. First, we must begin with the fact that Jesus was fully human and divine. If the goal for humans is to become Jesus the Christlike, then understanding how Jesus embodied true humanity has to be central to a Pan-Methodist soteriology. To this end, Jesus struggled against notions of just-us that were culturally defined, such as gender, class, and ethnicity. Jesus' struggle against just-us issues within Jewish society has a simultaneity that should inform our understanding of what it means to be truly human. Jesus works at the personal and systemic level at the same time.

For example, Jesus healed a person with a withered hand on the Sabbath, which was contrary to the law; but just as important is Jesus' willingness to come into physical contact with someone who Jewish society would consider not whole or unclean. Jesus addresses the concern of the individual while struggling against a class distinction that separated those with certain infirmities from those who were considered without blemish. Jesus is often deconstructing and reconstructing at the same time. Jesus deconstructs preconceived ideas about wholeness that created class distinctions while reconstructing the manner in which the man with the withered hand related to others in the community. To be truly human is an effort to deconstruct just-us issues while reconstructing how we form community.

Jesus uses a similar strategy when directly challenging those who are a part of the power structure. When Jesus is brought before Pontius Pilate and given a chance to refute the charges against him, Jesus' response points out Pilate's power as an individual and also his role within an oppressive system. Pilate represents the power structure oppressing the Jews, but he also has the authority as an individual to change the circumstances of Jesus' fate. Pilate tries to negotiate these two realities by claiming he finds no fault with Jesus and is willing to free Jesus if it is the will of the people. Handling Jesus' situation in this manner allows Pilate to maintain his standing with Rome and divorce himself from personal guilt. In other words, Pilate can argue he personally is not responsible for the injustice against Jesus because he offered the people an alternative.

The actions of Pilate are helpful for understanding some of the current dialogues related to race, class, and gender. Most Euro-Americans will admit that African Americans were mistreated in the past but argue things have changed and attempt to divorce themselves from the actions of the past. Cobb offers: "The practical meaning of this new whiteness, however, is repudiation of any responsibility for the continuing consequences of the earlier form of whiteness. Because these whites are not now advocating exclusion of blacks from public life, they suppose that the collective acts of whites in the past are none of their doing."[14]

In a way similar to Pilate's attempt to divorce himself from responsibility for the injustice against Jesus, many Euro-Americans attempt to divorce themselves from the responsibility of their ancestors. The same is true for the actions of some African American men against African American women. These men divorce themselves from their gender privilege and take no responsibility for the ongoing oppression of African American women.

To be truly human like Jesus means navigating the different roles we play in society in relation to others. Navigating between our roles as individuals and as members of a community creates different layers of power that we wield and to which we are responsible. What makes navigating these roles so challenging is we live in a culture that privileges the individual in a way that diminishes the importance of the common good. Even our brand of Christianity in America is more about what Jesus does for the individual (a form of just-us) and not about disclosing the layers of power we all struggle with as part of a community. A Pan-Methodist soteriological approach seeks to help people navigate between the personal and social in a way that discloses the layers of power by focusing on real bodies.

In addition to the need for embracing Jesus' full humanity as well as his divinity, Cone points us toward a different vision of the relationship between true humanity and justification. Jesus discloses the challenge Christians face when seeking to embody truly human lives in particular contexts. For the oppressed and the oppressor the challenge often takes the form of determining one's identity. In many instances, those in power determine or construct the oppressor's identity as well as the identity of the oppressed. For example, some men determine their value or humanity based on an identification of cultural definitions of maleness. Certainly, identifying with the oppressor can mean security for those in power and at times even for the disenfranchised, but this often leads to various forms of nonbeing (the opposite of being truly human). In terms of race, this means to be white not only creates security but also differentiates one from those who are nonwhite, or not truly human.[15]

If one, however, identifies with the oppressed, then it can mean the disclosure of that which is systemic, while unfortunately opening oneself up to being silenced by those in power. The risk of the faith for those who seek to be truly human is the act of disclosing injustices while realizing that this very act opens them up to being silenced. To embody what it means to be truly human in the way that Jesus did puts one on a path toward confronting those with power. This confrontation can lead to the ultimate act of silencing—death. At least this is what those with power seek.

Martin Luther King, Jr. realized this risk of faith as he worked for equality during the Civil Rights movement. In fact, in his last speech, "I See the Promised Land," he talks about the risk of faith in his own life and ministry. King was killed the next day in Memphis. King was far from perfect (he was often androcentric), but he is an individual who worked to embody true humanity in a fashion similar to Jesus. King realized that seeking to disclose injustices opened him up to being silenced. King was willing to take on this risk of faith because he understood it was not his work, but God's work.

There are other examples from history of people who were willing to take the risk of faith knowing that the result could be their permanent silence. It is unfair to say these individuals had a death wish, but they did understand the systems opposing them were trying to silence them by any means necessary. When individuals are in these roles, it would be disingenuous to claim they are not sacrificing at some level. Not only King but also women like Rosa Parks and Fannie Lou Hamer gave their bodies to disclose the injustices occurring in America. Giving the self in this way is a risk of faith that those who oppose systemic oppression are willing to take. The willingness of Jesus to oppose the systemic ills of first-century Palestine has a lot to do with African American women and men doing the same years later.

For Christians, Jesus' embodiment of true humanity ends up in the ultimate attempt of silencing—silencing God. Not only is God silenced; God is silenced in a violent manner. Therefore, the cross is problematic for many Christians and non-Christians because it represents a bloody death and highlights human sacrifice. As a result, the opposition by some to a more traditional understanding of justification is that it promotes these images of Jesus the Christ. The question of salvation gets interpreted through a lens that focuses on the violent and sacrificial death of Jesus the Christ.

It is possible to broaden how Pan-Methodists understand justification, without diminishing some of the central claims by some traditionalists. Collins, interpreting Wesley, says three things about how we should understand justification.[16] First, Christ is the proper object of our faith, and faith in God is through Christ.[17] Second, justifying faith is more than a rational assent; it includes a "disposition of the heart."[18] Third, justifying faith is the means by which humans are saved from eternal death and are restored to life.[19] Although other Wesleyan scholars may nuance Collins on particular issues, they agree with his overall interpretation of Wesley on justification. Justification is a faith in Christ involving head and heart; it is the means by which humans are saved from eternal death.

A Pan-Methodist approach has not altered in any way the first two points Collins makes. Jesus the Christ is the proper object of our faith as we seek to navigate the different roles we play in society. Navigating these roles requires more than rational ways of knowing and doing; navigating these roles requires embodying who Jesus was as fully human. The real question is, *Does a Pan-Methodist soteriological approach alter an understanding of justifying faith as the means by which humans are saved from eternal death?* While not altering this understanding of justifying grace, a Pan-Methodist approach broadens it significantly. A Pan-Methodist approach makes explicit the ways in which Jesus' death and resurrection are always focusing on the simultaneity of transforming individuals and systemic structures.

Beginning with the death and resurrection of Jesus the Christ diminishes the importance of how Jesus embodied what it means to be human. The power of God acting for humanity is not one act on the cross and the rest just window dressing. The power of God coming into human form has significance for the way in which we are saved from eternal death and are restored to life. Jesus discloses the importance of this struggle in life and in the reality that to truly embody this form of faith is a risk that can lead to the cross. The attempt to silence Jesus and others willing to take this risk of faith will always fail because the Word of God overcomes the power of death and refuses to be silenced.

Because the Word could not be silenced, it is possible to be saved from eternal death; but more importantly it is possible to have life. The overcoming of eternal death and a restoration to life require a willingness to risk like Jesus, with the knowledge that those in power will attempt to silence one. The cross exposes the inability of human constructs to silence the Word of God. We are justified by a risk of faith through Christ because that risk demonstrates that we accept that Jesus the Christ has overcome death and can restore us to life. It is not simply a personal restoration but includes the struggle for justice and not just-us. Baker-Fletcher describes this broader understanding of justification in this manner: "Divine, justifying grace in the Word/Wisdom of God receives the persuaded, convicted hearts of the world to free them from hatred and unnecessary violence. The Word/Wisdom of God frees, justifies, and redeems those who desire to participate in divine love so that they may love others."[20]

Justification through the risk of faith means being redeemed so that we can embody true humanity, which is God freeing us to love as Jesus loved. Redemption is a divine act—a divine act that begins with Jesus' life and continues with the attempt to silence the Word of God, which is impossible.

In this sense, justification is a part of God's plan of salvation and is predicated on human conversion. As humans, we must be converted to a new understanding of who we are as individuals and as part of the communion of believers. Cone claims this about conversion: "Fellowship with God is the beginning and the end of human liberation. The liberated person is the one who encounters God in faith, that is, in conviction and trust that one's true humanity is actualized in God. This vertical dimension of faith is the essential response to the gospel and is thus the heart of liberation's meaning from the human side."[21]

Thinking about conversion in this manner connects to what it means to be truly human, because it is when we confront our own cultural accommodations and those of others as Jesus did that we begin to live as transformed people. If we are justified, then this confrontation is not rooted in violence or silencing the other like oppressors attempt to do but rather is done in love.

Collins develops even further the importance of conversion as a signal of being countercultural when he claims:

> Though theological conversion is often painted by its critics as "individualistic," it actually tends to be both far more personal and countercultural in its outworking than some have imagined.... Jesus' proclamation that unless a person is born again he or she shall not enter the kingdom of God confronted the religious status quo of Israel at its very roots and called for both honesty, in terms of painful recognition of need, as well as humility, with respect to being open to change. But all of this was hardly an invitation to individualism then as now. On the contrary, it was a call that entailed great *personal* depth and at times significant social dislocation.[22]

Collins correctly interprets the simultaneity of Jesus' embodiment of true humanity. I place a greater emphasis on the need for social transformation within the United States because of the history surrounding race, class, and gender—particularly the history within Methodism concerning these issues. The point is that justification requires being converted in a manner that challenges personal and systemic ills.

If those involved in the Jena Six situation had understood their humanity in the way I outlined above, then this involvement might have altered blatant commitments to just-us and meant a move toward justice. On the one side, a commitment to justice means individuals taking ownership of the layered structures of power within the culture and their place within that structure. On the other side, a commitment to justice means the struggle for justice requires opposing systemic evil as a practice of ministry that moves communities toward a real sense of wholeness. To be truly human means deconstructing the ways in which we promote nonbeing with an eye toward reconstructing what true humanity looks like.

The Wounds of Jesus

One of the interesting pericopes in the Gospel of John (20:24-29) is when Jesus appears to the disciples and shows Thomas the wounds on his body. In fact, Jesus has Thomas physically touch the areas where the nails entered his hand and where the sword pierced his side. This particular section is important for an embodied soteriological approach because it connects the struggle for justice with what we often term *sanctification*. Sanctification is about recovering the holiness of Jesus the Christ. Being holy like Jesus the Christ is not about living a life constrained by legal parameters but rather living a life dedicated to becoming whole in the way that Jesus the Christ embodied holiness. We begin the process of becoming whole on this side of heaven by living out our salvation by loving God and our neighbor.

A Pan-Methodist approach to soteriology understands the process of becoming whole in light of John 20:24-29. Attempts to silence the Word always fail, but this does not mean the wounds magically disappear. The living out of salvation on this side of heaven, for those committed to embodying Jesus the Christ's struggle for humanity, necessitates living with visible wounds. The idea of becoming like Jesus the Christ should not be equated with a form of perfectionism that erases all problems or blemishes. Becoming like Jesus the Christ means we work toward wholeness with the full realization that the problems of personal and communal sin do not magically disappear.

Baker-Fletcher tells a story about a person named Anthony that helps illumine the importance of thinking about sanctification (perfection) from an embodied approach. She describes how Anthony was "diagnosed with *systemic lupus erythematosus*" at the age of sixteen and was originally only given nine more years to live.[23] When Anthony failed to be healed in a manner that some of his more charismatic friends prescribed, they believed he had done something to oppose God. The implication was that Anthony would be healed of lupus if his faith were strong.[24] I agree with Baker-Fletcher that understanding faith and the Christian journey in this manner takes us in the wrong direction. The life of holiness is not about God working through the Holy Spirit to magically take away those things influencing our bodies, but it is about God through the Holy Spirit making us more like Jesus the Christ, who after the Resurrection returned with visible signs of woundedness.

Anthony did experience miracles in his life. He celebrated his fiftieth birthday in 2005 and continues to live with lupus even though it means he now requires a wheelchair.[25] Anthony continues to live daily with the reality of his lupus, but this reality points to the power of the Holy Spirit to work in his life. Baker-Fletcher makes this observation about the fear of disabilities as it relates to the work of the Holy Spirit:

> There is evidence of the power of the Holy Spirit in one's life when one responds to persons with physical or mental challenges, not in condescension, but with respect and joy in the goodness of God in the land of the living. All too often there is failure to see the gift that God has given to those with visible handicaps. An unwitting, faithless fear of the vulnerability of the human body emerges in its place. This leads to some of the unacknowledged obstacles that people with disabilities face everyday: pity, arrogance, and patronizing attitudes. In the power of the Holy Spirit, one responds instead with an attitude of thankfulness for abundant life.[26]

If we follow Baker-Fletcher's logic as it relates to disabilities, then it should be no surprise that many of our descriptions of sanctification embrace able-bodiedness and not the reality of Jesus the Christ's appearing as wounded after the Resurrection. Resurrecting power is equated with a form of perfectionism that is dangerous for individuals and communities because it seeks to remove the wounds of the cross. A better understanding of sanctification should move us toward embracing the visible wounds of the cross; thus the journey toward likeness with Jesus the Christ is reinterpreted both individually and communally.

For an individual to become like Jesus the Christ the Holy Spirit must work through a person in such a way that he or she becomes vulnerable like Jesus. A willingness to show and share one's wounds with another is contrary to what we practice in American society. A sports analogy may be helpful to make this point. In basketball, if the star player hurts her wrist during the game, then her team will attempt to conceal the injury if at all possible. Her team does not want the other team to know they are vulnerable because of her injury. As individuals, we operate the same way and hide our wounds from others because we do not want them to see our vulnerability. In reality, to become like Jesus the Christ we should be opening ourselves up to God and others.

Opening ourselves up to God and others is precisely what we are called to do as we renew the image of God in our lives. Theodore Runyon argues that the best way to understand the process of renewing the image of God in our lives that occurs in sanctification (perfection) requires looking to how God loves us. Runyon writes:

> The best starting point for reinterpreting and reappropriating Wesley's doctrine of Christian perfection, therefore, is the *perfection of God's love* as we receive it from Christ through the Holy Spirit. But in rethinking this doctrine it is important to focus first of all not on our own perfection but on the perfection of *that which we receive*. God's love is perfect. There is no more ultimate, more complete, more holy, more self-giving love than that which is directed toward us from the divine Giver. This love is sheer *grace*, and it is the love that God shares with those called to be God's image. We receive and participate in perfect love.[27]

Runyon supports a Pan-Methodist approach by emphasizing that we should understand sanctification from the perspective of Jesus the Christ. To be renewed in the image of God and be made whole is about mirroring the love of Jesus the Christ.[28] To be clear, I am suggesting this love starts with the wounds of Jesus the Christ, who embodies what it means to be vulnerable. To be renewed as individuals into the moral image of Jesus the Christ requires living out mercy and justice, not from the perspective of hierarchal power but from a perspective that begins with embodying vulnerability—which is empowering. To be renewed in the moral image of Jesus the Christ requires humility and an understanding of love that is different from the usual hierarchal understandings of love.[29] Mirroring God's love requires both seeing the humility of Jesus the Christ and reflecting this to others.

The journey toward likeness with Jesus the Christ is not individualistic, because it is done within a community. Mirroring God's love assumes a community in which this love is reflected. The challenge is mirroring God's love and living a life vulnerable to God and others in a culture that prioritizes just-us thinking. We are formed in a culture that privileges race, gender, and class distinctions, making it difficult to love in a genuine manner those different from us. Cobb describes the challenge of creating community, given that he is a white male: "I am not an individual separate from the communities that have formed me. I am what I am by the internalization of others. Many, if not most, of those others have had, and acted on, a white identity. Internalizing them has made me white. It is from that white perspective that I see others. What has been socially constructed plays a large role in constituting my identity."[30] Simply making the claim that one is a Christian or a Methodist does not negate the socially constructed identities we all develop. Our identities are formed within a cultural context that values and devalues other identities.

The logic of Jesus the Christ appearing with the wounds of the cross acts as a constant reminder to all of us that communal transformation is not easy and comes with a price. The goal of perfecting love in a culture that privileges gender, race, and class (to name a few) may resemble a love more for one's privilege than a love that is countercultural. This is because Methodists (Christians) often focus on the renewal of the moral image of God and neglect the renewal of the political image of God. It is the political image that most directly influences how we relate to one another and creation.

For a Pan-Methodist soteriology, the renewal of the political image of God moves beyond the typical Wesleyan understanding of humans mirroring God's stewardship here on the earth.[31] The renewal of the political image within an American context is fundamentally about mirroring God's relationship within the Trinity as a model for community. The renewal of the political image is not about investing humans with power over the earth but is about liberating others to become an active part of the community. If we are seeking to be made like Jesus the Christ, then liberation is more than a spiritual catchphrase; it requires embodying the very struggle of Jesus' life, ministry, and resurrection.

The renewal of the political image of God works in conjunction with the renewal of the moral image. This means that as humans we are being renewed in the moral and political image of God simultaneously, and it is not possible to have one without the other. The hope of living a transformed life and continuing God's work of transformation within a particular context is based upon our renewal in both the moral and political images. Although love is the goal in both cases, it is not a love that resembles current cultural privileging; it is a love that embodies the hope of God resurrecting Jesus the Christ with the wounds and the vulnerability of living with wounds as we move from just-us to justice in our relationships with one another.

Baker-Fletcher captures some of the sentiment of a Pan-Methodist understanding of sanctification when she writes, "The sanctifying grace of God, in the power of the Holy Spirit, heals the wounds inflicted by evil actions and perfects the love of followers of the Word/Wisdom of God to make them whole."[32] The idea of the wounds being healed is important, but this does not mean the wounds disappear. Becoming whole within a

Pan-Methodist model of sanctification agrees with the healing of the wounds we suffer in the struggle against the systemic power structures opposed to God, but realizes the wounds do not simply disappear as we move toward wholeness. This means our struggle for wholeness is real and is more than spiritual—it is an embodied struggle. It also points us toward renewal into the full image of Jesus the Christ, which includes both moral and political renewal. God is working to renew all of creation, and we participate in God's work of renewal when we embody the struggle for justice and move beyond just-us issues within our lives and communities.

Attempting to move beyond the deep wounds of just-us in the Jena Six situation will be difficult. Deep wounds have existed in Jena for a long time and the incident reopened those wounds and exposed them to national scrutiny. The wounds are not going to magically disappear as the town seeks healing, but the wounds can become an entry for a deeper relationship with God and neighbor that embodies the struggle for justice of Jesus the Christ. Deconstructing just-us communal relationships will not be easy because systemic evil is real and it is working to silence those voices seeking true justice. God, through the Holy Spirit, is always working through people and communities to bring about a true transformation that alters the very way we live life and relate to one another. In Jena, this transformative process is possible only if individuals and communities are willing to be vulnerable in such a way that others can truly touch their wounds.

A Pan-Methodist Soteriology

This Pan-Methodist approach is grounded in African American and Wesleyan soteriological approaches, which in some ways constricts it to those disciplines, but my intent is not to be so constricted that a Pan-Methodist approach is simply redundant of the other two. There are three reasons that a Pan-Methodist approach offers insights into African American and Wesleyan scholarship that can encourage them to rethink soteriological issues.

First, because a Pan-Methodist approach focuses on embodiment, it maintains a contextual emphasis while having universal application. One of the critiques against some African American and Wesleyan soteriological approaches is the way in which they are contextualized into American Methodist culture. A Pan-Methodist approach creates a method for some African American and Wesleyan scholars to rethink their soteriological approaches in light of the historical and ongoing rifts in Methodism. This requires integrating the concerns and insights of the broader Methodist community into their soteriologies. If some African American and Wesleyan scholars broaden their soteriological emphasis, then their soteriologies become more universal because they are more reflective of American Methodism and not simply their constituency.

Second, a Pan-Methodist soteriological approach seeks to maintain the unique significance of the cross while honoring some feminist or womanist critiques. Certainly what I am suggesting is not sufficient, but my intent is to open a space within a Pan-Methodist approach that continues the dialogue. The fact that some in the culture are attempting to silence those advocating for justice is a reality that Jesus faced and we face. The fact is that those advocating for justice often end up experiencing violence at the hands of just-us proponents. Because Jesus the Christ is fully human and divine, Jesus is the ultimate disclosure of the ways in which just-us proponents attempt to silence the Word of God. Fortunately there is another reality with Jesus the Christ that gives us all hope in our struggle for justice. God's Word is eternal and was resurrected from the grave, which means salvation is possible for all of us as we struggle against just-us and for justice. Moving toward justice and not just-us often includes sacrifice by those who believe in the struggle of Jesus the Christ, but it does not advocate for surrogacy that imitates human disempowering relationships.

Third, a Pan-Methodist soteriological approach perceives the wounds of Jesus the Christ as the key to sanctification. The ideal of perfecting love is central to a Wesleyan understanding of sanctification, but if we follow Jesus the Christ we should realize this is not a cheap form of love. The attempt to build relationships with others that are based upon justice can lead to the type of wounds Jesus the Christ experienced. As we recover the image of God, these wounds do heal, but the marks of the wounds do not disappear. To renew the moral and political image of God means opening ourselves to others who may have hurt us deeply even as we try to build community with them. This opening up is not done naively, where power relationships remain the same. It can only be accomplished where the political image as understood from a liberationist's perspective is being renewed.

Many Christians, and Methodists in particular, may agree with some of this proposal for a Pan-Methodist soteriology; nevertheless, there are some valid critiques of what I am proposing. One such critique is that I am pulling together many schools of thought in a way that does not fully represent the nuanced theology of any particular school. I am working with black, feminist, Wesleyan, and womanist thinkers, and I cannot do justice to the variety and depth of these schools in this project. I do believe the thinkers I have incorporated from the various schools help paint a picture for what a more integrated approach to Methodist soteriology can look like, thereby encouraging a more integrated approach in Methodist studies.

Another valid critique is that I limit the just-us issues throughout this book and especially in this chapter. This is a valid critique because my focus is mainly race, with gender and class as my two other just-us concerns. The goal is to develop a soteriology that can address various just-us issues by using the framework I have developed, a framework that is not limited to race, class, and gender. Individuals who work with other just-us concerns will better judge if I accomplished this task, but I do recognize we live in a culture replete with just-us issues.

Finally, some individuals like the possibilities that a Pan-Methodist soteriology holds for Methodists in the United States but wonder if this approach really can make a difference for the various Methodist constituencies. If we move in the direction I am suggesting, then how will this change the way the various Methodist denominations or other groups with long histories of disempowerment relate to one another? This is the topic of the next chapter as I explore the possibilities for developing new relationships toward a just community.

CHAPTER 6

ENGAGING FRIENDSHIP

The language of friendship carries with it theological and ethical baggage dating back to Aristotle.[1] Notwithstanding this baggage, the idea of friendship still implies a relationship that moves beyond mere acquaintance toward some form of mutuality with another. This mutuality is based upon seeing the other and hearing the other without having to re-create the other into one's own image. Developing this type of friendship is difficult for individuals and even more difficult for communities.

The various denominations within Pan-Methodism should move toward modeling a form of friendship that resembles the mutuality described above, if they are to live out, with any conviction, an authentic soteriology. This means Euro-American Methodists have to develop a different understanding of loving one's neighbor that recognizes their reliance upon whiteness. Perpetuating whiteness as the basis for establishing relationships assumes all parties are white and negates the possibility for true friendship with nonwhites. It also means African Americans have to develop a different understanding of loving one's neighbor that incorporates new biblical models for community. Both the liberation and survival model rely too heavily upon complete physical separation from Euro-Americans, which is unrealistic within the United States.

This chapter will offer a model for developing engaging friendships among the various denominations within Pan-Methodism, and it is a model that has implications for other groups struggling with racial just-us. The chapter begins by exploring models of relating to others developed from Mark Twain's *The Adventures of Huckleberry Finn*, which represents some of the difficulties with reconciliation considerations. Then the chapter proposes a model of friendship based upon Alice Walker's *The Color Purple*, which better represents mutuality toward another. The chapter concludes with some broader implications for the Pan-Methodist community if it lives out an embodied soteriology within the United States.

Why Reconciliation Efforts Rarely Work

The goal of reconciliation between individuals or communities who have experienced separation seems appropriate. The idea behind reconciliation is to bring together again individuals or communities who were separated. This implies that at some point a relationship existed between the two. For example, two people who have been friends since elementary school get into a fight as college roommates and go their separate ways, but five years later decide to reestablish the relationship. The ability to reconcile is predicated in part on a prior relationship existing between the parties.

Theologically, one can argue that, because we are created in the image of God, all humans have a starting point for reconciliation. In other words, reconciliation in this instance is not based on a prior human relationship, like the example of the elementary school friends but is rather based on our common heritage as God's children. If one uses this logic, then regardless of whether a prior human relationship existed, reconciliation is possible. Reconciliation is based on a deeper heritage than the relationships we establish as humans.

The problem with both nontheological and theological reconciliation efforts is the assumption implied but never openly stated, namely that all parties being reconciled are equal partners. The two friends are able to reconcile because there is not a great disparity in the power dynamic between them. For example, they share a common background or socioeconomic status (for example, race, class, or gender), making reconciliation easier. Conversely, reconciliation between nonequals or those perceived as nonequals is difficult because one party sets the terms for reconciling. In Mark Twain's classic novel *The Adventures of Huckleberry Finn*, Huckleberry Finn's "Pap" returns to "reconcile" with his son, but the terms for reconciling include that Huckleberry turn over the money he has come into recently.[2] Huckleberry's Pap, because he is an adult, is setting the terms for reconciling or being in Huckleberry's life—one suspects until he spends all of the money. The point is that a power differential exists, which makes reconciliation one-sided in favor of Pap.

Theologically, it is one thing to claim everyone is a child of God, but it is another to live this reality. Even if we are all accepted and reconciled to God by God, the mirroring of God's actions by humans often gets tangled in just-us power differentials. For example, reconciliation between African Americans and Euro-Americans usually favors Euro-Americans because of the power differential that exists in the United States. James Cone articulates in the following manner the power differential we face in reconciling:

> On the human side, reconciliation means that we blacks must accept our new existence by struggling against all who try to make us slaves. We must refuse to let whites define the terms of reconciliation. Instead, we must participate in God's revolutionary activity in the world by changing the political, economic, and social structures so that the distinctions between rich and poor, oppressed and oppressors, are no longer a reality among people.[3]

Even theologically a problem exists on the human side of reconciliation, because the way in which we represent God defines the terms of reconciliation consciously or unconsciously in terms of just-us. The challenge for those on the underside of the equation is not to let those in power define reconciliation in their favor.

Cone describes well the issues related to those in power wielding it in a way that enables them to maintain their advantages. Certainly individuals still exist within the church who seek to maintain their advantage over others by wielding power to suit their ends. Two other realities, just as troubling and just as much in need of being addressed, also exist in the church. First, many Euro-Americans who believe they are living out their calling to love their neighbor as themselves are perpetuating the power differential between the races. These individuals are not purposely using whiteness to their advantage, but the way in which they relate to people of color usually ends up perpetuating the advantages of whiteness.

Second, some African Americans attempt to counter the power differential between the races by developing similar models in a context that does not readily support complete physical separation from oppressors. The challenge is daunting because both liberation and survival models suggest some degree of self-determination. The problem is relying on biblical models that promote complete physical separation and not simply isolated incidents of separation. The difference is that the former suggest a complete break with the oppressor, while the latter propose restructuring the shape and meaning of community for oppressed and oppressor.

The issue in either scenario is power. As long as Hagar and Ishmael were in the oppressor's house, their ability to determine the ethos of the house was restricted. It was not until they were kicked out and on their own that they were able to create an ethos for a different type of society. The truth is that breaking away from one's oppressor not only creates physical freedom but also a different form of epistemological freedom. When Hagar was kicked out of her oppressor's house for good, she was not only physically free; she understood freedom differently than when her decisions were based upon the possibility of repercussions from Abraham and Sarah. This does not mean there were no repercussions for the decisions she made when she was physically away from her oppressor. The epistemology involved in decisions made while living in the midst of your oppressor are very different from those made while completely separated from your oppressor. Therefore, for African Americans within the United States, liberation and survival are usually a balancing act between dealing with the ethos of society and constructing an alternate ethos within the African American community. This balancing act means African Americans never experience complete physical or epistemological freedom in the United States because the ethos of oppression permeates the structures in which we live and make decisions.

Mark Twain's *The Adventures of Huckleberry Finn* provides a lens for us to understand the roots both of African Americans living a balancing act and of Euro-Americans consciously or unconsciously seeking a power advantage that perpetuates whiteness. A great portion of the novel revolves around the relationship between Huckleberry and Jim, who at the beginning of the novel is a runaway slave. By focusing on the adventures of Huck and Jim, it is possible to sketch out some theological insights related to the challenges of reconciliation in: (1) those completely opposed to the idea (Pap), (2) those who consciously use their whiteness (Tom), (3) those perpetuating whiteness at times unconsciously (Huckleberry), and (4) those living a balancing act (Jim).

Pap is racist and tries to influence Huck to be the same. Pap tells Huck about an encounter he has with a free African American[4] male that upsets him greatly. Pap reports:

> Oh, yes, this is a wonderful govment, wonderful. Why looky here. There was a free nigger there from Ohio—a mulatter, most as white as a white man. . . . They said he was a p'fessor in a college, and could talk all kinds of languages, and knowed everything. And that ain't the wust. They said he could *vote* when he was at home. Well that let me out.

> Thinks I, what is the country a-coming to? It was 'lection day, and I was just about to go and vote myself if I warn't too drunk to get there; but when they told me there was a state in this country where they'd let that nigger vote, I drawed out.[5]

In the above statement Pap lets the reader in on his discomfort with race and class issues. He believes that a poor white male should have more rights than an educated black male. Pap discounts the fact that the African American male is a professor and can speak several languages, because what is essential is whiteness.

For Pap, African Americans are nonbeings and Euro-Americans are the only real people. There is a clear power differential between blacks and whites that maintains Euro-Americans as the masters and African Americans as the slaves. Cone argues that communication leading toward reconciliation is not possible in a hierarchal relationship—masters and slaves.[6] Those claiming to be masters believe their authority comes from whiteness, implying that God made them superior to nonwhites. The subject of reconciliation is inauthentic in this case because there is no consideration given to changing the status quo. Even today, Euro-Americans believing they are superior to African Americans cannot truly engage in authentic discussions about reconciliation.

In the novel, Tom Sawyer is an interesting character because he decides to join forces with Huck in helping Jim. The problem is Tom still operates with a white consciousness that perceives blacks as inferior. Tom's perception of blacks is different from Pap's because he is willing to free Jim, whereas Pap does not believe African Americans should be free. Pap tells Huck at one point:

> And to see the cool way of that nigger—why, he wouldn't 'a' give me the road if I hadn't shoved him out o' the way. I says to the people, why ain't this nigger put up at auction and sold?—that's what I want to know. And what do you reckon they said? Why, they said he couldn't be sold till he'd been in the state six months, and he hadn't been there that long yet.[7]

Pap is upset at the idea that anyone of color could be free and not living in her or his proper place as a slave, and he is opposed to any form of freedom for African Americans.

Tom's perpetuating whiteness is in a way different from Pap's, because Tom is not opposed to freeing some African Americans; but it must be done on his terms. The sad truth is that freeing Jim is a game for Tom and not perceived as the serious matter it should be concerning human life. By reading between the lines we also get a glimpse of how Tom perpetuates a form of whiteness that promotes the idea that Euro-Americans know what is best and should determine the fate of others. Tom suggests that Jim will be better off depending on him and Huck (and eventually their children) for freedom than he would be if he were actually free. Although the idea of freedom is not egregious to Tom, he sets the parameters in such a way that he consciously always maintains control. Huck's comments about Tom's intent to free Jim are very telling at this point in the novel. Huck records:

> Tom was in high spirits. He said it was the best fun he ever had in his life, and the most intellectural; and said if he only could see his way to it we would keep it up all the rest of our lives and leave Jim to our children to get out; for he believed Jim would come to like it better and better the more he got used to it. He said that in that way it could be strung out to as much as eighty year, and would be the best time on record. And he said it would make us all celebrated that had a hand in it.[8]

This perspective still exists today. Cone states, "Whether for us or against us, white people seem to think that they know what is best for the struggle."[9] Euro-Americans believe they have a superior understanding of African American circumstances, which gives them a right to determine our fate. At a certain level Tom probably believes he is doing the just thing in the way he is helping Jim, but the reality is Tom perpetuates white control, as Jim simply becomes a pawn for his amusement. Tom's interest is not in creating justice for Jim but in furthering his own agenda.

In fact, Tom is so pleased with his scheme that he fails to tell the others until the very end of the novel that Jim was already "liberated." Tom says to those who are holding Jim captive:

> Tom rose square up in bed, with his eye hot, and his nostrils opening and shutting like gills, and sings out to me: "They hain't no *right* to shut him up! *Shove*!—and don't you lose a minute. Turn him loose! He ain't no slave; he's as free as any cretur that walks this earth!"
>
> "What *does* the child mean?"
>
> "I mean every word I *say*, Aunt Sally, and if somebody don't go, I'll go. I've knowed him all his life, and so has Tom,[10] there. Old Miss Watson died two months ago, and she was ashamed she ever was going to sell him down the river, and *said* so; and she set him free in her will."

"Then what on earth did *you* want to set him free for, seeing he was already free?"

"Well that is a question, I must say; and just like women! Why, I wanted the adventure of it; and I'd 'a' waded neck-deep in blood to—goodness alive, Aunt Polly!"[11]

Three important theological themes are suggested in this passage. First, Tom claims Jim is as free as any other person on the earth. Tom's claim is inauthentic given his conscious effort to control Jim's life even to the degree of setting free an already free person. To be as free as any creature on the earth means the ability to flourish. The structures of society and those who control the structures restrict Jim's ability to flourish. Tom is a part of the group who controls the structures. Jim realizes this in the different way he addresses Tom in comparison to Huck. Jim refers to Tom as "Mars" (master), while Huck does not receive any such designation. Not only is Jim not as free as Tom, Huck is not as free as Tom, because a class distinction exists between the two.

Tom's standard determines the idea of freedom. As long as Jim is willing to live by the predetermined standard of freedom set for him, everything will be fine. Euro-Americans like Tom who consciously set parameters defining the existence of African Americans and other disenfranchised people, are not interested in true human flourishing. The goal is to perpetuate the structures of society in such a way that disenfranchised individuals can participate if they are willing to live unfulfilled lives. Karen Baker-Fletcher proposes that "it is precisely the decisions human and other creatures make that lead to experiences of perishing and becoming, death and life."[12] The decisions Tom and others with his mind-set are making lead to perishing for those who are disenfranchised, because the terms of freedom are disempowering.

Second, Tom tells his aunt that Jim was already set free in Miss Watson's will. This reinforces the notion that for Tom this is an "adventure" influencing someone else's well-being. Certainly this is a novel mainly about young boys and their adventures in life, but it also points to a deeper reality in American culture—the idea that one human has the right to determine the freedom of another. This is similar to the first point I made about freedom; however, the focus in this instance is the *imago dei*. Both Tom and Miss Watson never question the fact that they are setting free someone made in the image of God. They do not question this fact because Jim is viewed as property and not someone made in the image of God in the same manner as they.

To be made in the image of God is not only about who we are as individuals but also about who God is.[13] If God is for the oppressed, then God is in solidarity with the oppressed and not trying to oppress them further. Tom's logic and actions assume God is an oppressor because God's image is reflected in whiteness. For Tom, it is not incompatible with his understanding of whiteness to set Jim free, even though Miss Watson already did it in her will. More importantly, both Tom and Miss Watson misunderstand the connection between the expression of God's image in humanity and freedom. Freedom is not determined from the perspective of whiteness (oppressor) but rather is determined from the perspective of the oppressed.[14] Attempts by Euro-Americans to consciously reimagine themselves as God will always fail because God is with those being disenfranchised.

Third, Tom also characterizes the place of women as inferior to men in the way he replies to Aunt Polly's question about freedom by saying, "Just like women!" The overture is that Aunt Polly can never understand because she is female. Tom's explanation to his aunt is that he wanted adventure. The underlying assumption is that women are not suited for adventure because that is a role reserved for boys. The construction of whiteness in Euro-American males is so pervasive that in the chain of being, even white women are not created in God's image as white men are. As a result, the church and society develop structures that perpetuate whiteness and maleness. Even today, many Euro-American males consciously understand their advantages and use them to perpetuate their place in the chain of being.

Individuals with Tom's mind-set may be willing to reconcile, but it is an inauthentic reconciliation. The oppressor and not the oppressed will determine the terms for reconciling. The terms will perpetuate structures of whiteness that inhibit the ability of African Americans to flourish. This is why African Americans need to be cautious when discussing reconciliation, because if we move too quickly, such inauthentic reconciliation only ends up reinforcing the power differential between blacks and whites.[15] The fact that Euro-Americans talk about freedom is not grounds for entering into discussions on reconciliation. History has proved that some of them discuss freedom willingly with an understanding that they can perpetuate the status quo.

If Tom consciously was using whiteness to his advantage, then Huck is more ambiguous in his use of whiteness. Certainly Huck perceives the advantages he has because of his whiteness and that a power difference exists between him and Jim. For example, at one point in the novel Jim thinks they are about to arrive in a free town and starts planning on how he will unite his family.[16] Huck responds:

> It most froze me to hear such talk. He wouldn't ever dared to talk such talk in his life before. Just see what a difference it made in him the minute he judged he was about free. It was according to the old saying, "Give a nigger an inch and he'll take an ell." Thinks I, this is what comes of my not thinking. Here was this nigger, which I had as good as helped to run away, coming right out flat-footed and saying he would steal his children—children that belonged to a man I didn't even know; a man that hadn't ever done me no harm.[17]

This is a fascinating paragraph because in it Huck appears not to realize the inconsistency of his own thinking. On the one hand, Huck is angry with Jim because he perceives Jim as "stealing" his children from someone else in order to unite his family. On the other hand, Huck never questions that someone "stole" Jim and Jim's children. Although Huck is more ambiguous in his use of whiteness, it is clear that he understands the power differential that exists in society and the importance of his whiteness.

Huck, however, is different from Pap and Tom because he and Jim develop a relationship that at times goes beyond the usual constraints of society. At one point in the novel Huck plays a trick on Jim and Jim responds by saying, "Dat truck dah is *trash*; en trash is what people is dat puts dirt on de head er dey fren's en makes 'em ashamed."[18] Jim's statement is profound because it differentiates between authentic friendship and inauthentic friendship. Authentic friendship is based upon a mutuality that does not negate the personhood of another. Inauthentic friendship takes no heed of another and constantly places one party at the mercy of the other. The trick Huck played on Jim exemplified inauthentic friendship because it shamed Jim in a way that authentic friendship never would do.

Huck feels extremely low at this point and comments, "I could almost kissed *his* foot to get him to take it back."[19] This is just one example of where Huck struggles with what it means to be white. Huck understands the power differential between him and Jim, but at this moment that differential is not as important as their friendship. Huck finally says, "It was fifteen minutes before I could work myself up to go and humble myself to a nigger; but I done it, and I warn't ever sorry for it afterward, neither. I didn't do him no more mean tricks, and I wouldn't done that one of I'd 'a' knowed it would make him feel that way."[20]

In his own way Huck has come to terms with his whiteness and repents for his actions. Baker-Fletcher argues, "One may experience the power of divine love as a warm flame of comfort, when one is sinned against, or as a forge in which one experiences the pain he or she has caused others when one is the sinner."[21] Huck experienced the pain that his intentional actions caused Jim. The reality of this experience (if we take it to be authentic) is that Huck begins to perceive the humanity of Jim in a different manner. This does not negate the power differential that exists between the two, and it does not negate Huck's conscious acceptance of his whiteness. It does point to the possibility of a different reality that moves closer to Jim's understanding of how friends relate to one another than the societal structures Huck is called to perpetuate.

We can learn from Jim and Huck that mutuality does not come easy and that the very structures of society work against it. In the novel, when Huck and Jim are alone the relationship has a different sensibility about it than when they are with others. The truth is Huck probably would not have repented (humbled himself) to Jim in the presence of other white people. This is why developing authentic friendship is so difficult and reconciliation is a very last step. The ability to publicly repent and then live a new life based upon one's repentance often requires more of us than we are willing to risk.[22]

At the end of the novel we learn just how strong the ethos of societal structures are when Jim is captured as a runaway slave. Huck reports:

> They cussed Jim considerble, though and give him a cuff or two side the head once in a while, but Jim never said nothing, and he never let on to know me, and they took him to the same cabin, and put his own clothes on him, and chained him again, and not to no bed-leg this time, but to a big staple drove into the bottom log, and chained his hands, too, and both legs, and said he warn't to have nothing but bread and water to eat after this till his owner come, or he was sold at auction.[23]

This paragraph is telling because we get insight into Huck's struggle to perpetuate whiteness over against standing up for Jim. Standing up for Jim in this situation will mean telling others he has developed a friendly relationship with an African male. By staying quiet, he protects his station in society and is only perceived as an interested onlooker. Jim aids Huck in this process by never letting on that the two know each other.

Even though Jim and Huck have been through a lot together, and in some ways Jim provides the guidance that Pap never did, Huck stays quiet during Jim's time of need.

Huck is a more ambiguous character than Tom and Pap because there are instances when he does come to Jim's aid, like when he lies to slave trackers to protect him.[24] Although Huck perpetuates whiteness, he also has moments of standing with Jim and aiding him in his pursuit of freedom. The challenge for Huck and many Euro-Americans today is living a life that resists giving in to whiteness. This requires a conversion experience. Cone writes, "When whites undergo the true experience of conversion wherein they die to whiteness and are reborn anew in order to struggle against white oppression and for the liberation of the oppressed, there is a place for them in the black struggle of freedom."[25]

Dying to whiteness is easier said than done, as Huck exemplifies throughout the novel. Society is structured in such a way that resisting whiteness is almost impossible. To stay silent and maintain one's station in life is always an option when someone is white. For Euro-Americans trying to make a difference, it is still an uphill battle because a just-us mentality permeates our communities. Luther Smith makes observations about a Euro-American couple who thought living in intentional community with African Americans could make a difference in race relations:

> They were disappointed but wiser. Racism and its consequences have not been perpetuated because people do not smile and wave enough. The causes of racism are a tangled knot of complicated social, political, economic, and religious forces. The couple now understood this and realized that not only were they unprepared for their neighborhood's harsh realities, but they needed another environment in which to reconsider the meaning of Christian commitment.[26]

I am not privy to all that the couple encountered, but Smith's comments support the notion that resisting whiteness and what that entails in the United States is easier said than done. The couple was not prepared for the reality of confronting their whiteness and the privileges connected to it. The couple underwent a conversion type of experience that helped them understand some of the underlying issues related to race relations. The power of Cone's understanding of conversion is that he helps us delineate what is gained and lost. What is lost is the privilege of whiteness, but what is gained is siding with the disenfranchised in their fight for justice. The challenge for this couple was acting on what was gained while still resisting whiteness. The truth is, what is gained requires an ongoing commitment to transformation, making many unwilling to convert.

Even individuals like Huck, who are willing to aid African Americans in the struggle for justice, often are not true converts. They are unwilling to completely give up the privileges of whiteness, and they opt to live ambiguous lives that ultimately perpetuate the status quo. True reconciliation is not possible in this instance because the power differential still exists between the races. The difference in this case is that the use of power is more ambiguous than it is among those who consciously perpetuate whiteness.

The challenge is magnified even when some Euro-Americans attempt to resist their whiteness by living in intentional community with African Americans. They discover that loving their neighbors is a more daunting task than they imagined. The reality is that the attempt to love their neighbors as they love themselves means a love of whiteness. It is not a conscious effort to love whiteness, but such love is the ethos that permeates all of society and the ways Euro-Americans made meaning out of life. Resisting the love of self in this case means being born anew to a new reality that focuses on the other and not the self. In the United States, we are a long way from a reality that resists whiteness. Therefore, talk of reconciliation is premature at all levels of society, including within Pan-Methodism.

The other side of the equation is Jim's reaction to the different ways in which he experienced just-us. Jim is representative of African Americans in the novel to the extent that he attempts to balance getting away from a system of oppression while seeking the freedom of others—his family. I am not suggesting Jim embodies a liberation or survival model, but that he illumines the balancing act many African Americans face in trying to flourish individually while staying committed to helping others in the community. I named this balancing act in chapter 4 as a form of double consciousness, because it forces African Americans to live in two worlds without ever being comfortable in either.[27] If African Americans could physically separate themselves from their oppressor for good, then this could resolve the tension in one way. The other option is to simply accept the role the oppressor created for us, which would resolve the tension in another way. Making a choice to live with the tension means accepting the reality of not physically separating and not accepting the role created for us.

Jim confronts the latter option when he overhears his owner, Miss Watson, talking about selling him for eight hundred dollars. Jim tells Huck what he overheard:

> Well, you see, it 'uz dis way. Ole missus—dat's Miss Watson—she pecks on me all de time, en treats me pooty rough, but she awluz said she wouldn't sell me down to Orleans. But I noticed dey wuz a nigger trader roun' de place considable lately, en I begin to git oneasy. Well, one night I creeps to de do', pooty late, en de do' warn't quite shet, en I hear old missus tell de wider she gwyne to sell me down to Orleans, but she didn' want to, but she could git eight hund'd dollars for me, en it 'uz sich a big stack o' money she couldn' resis'.[28]

It is at this point in the novel that Jim decides to run away and not let his oppressor control his fate. Jim decides to take his chances in the wilderness, where he could escape the possibility of being sold and experience a sacred space away from his oppressor.[29] Certainly the wilderness also meant dealing with uncertainty such as trying to find food and avoiding slave trackers, but given a choice between surviving in the wilderness or staying in oppression, Jim chooses the wilderness.[30]

Obviously, Jim's escape to a sacred space is interrupted by Huck, who after faking his own death has run away to the same island as Jim. This does not deter Jim's intent of making it to a free state with the hopes of one day returning for his family. Huck reports Jim's conversation:

> He was saying how the first thing he would do when he got to a free state he would go to saving up money and never spend a single cent, and when he got enough he would buy his wife, which was on a farm close to where Miss Watson lived; and they would both work to buy the two children, and if their master wouldn't sell them, they'd get an Ab'litionist to go and steal them.[31]

An important theological point is imbedded in Jim's comments. Jim embodies the idea that there is no freedom until all are free.[32] It is unfair to mistake Jim for Harriet Tubman, who risked her life for others not related to her, but Jim is not interested in saving himself and forgetting about the rest of his family. Jim's willingness to risk his life in order to make sure the rest of his family is safe cannot be stressed too much. Jim simply could make his way to a free state and be content with his freedom. The measure of freedom is not based upon what we achieve individually, but is connected to what the entire oppressed community experiences.[33]

This presents a challenge for African Americans within the United States who are committed to making a way in the same land as their oppressor. It is one thing to make a way that embodies a new vision of community that enables all individuals to flourish, and quite another to simply accept the vision of community created for you. African Americans have to deal with the reality of continuous physical contact with the oppressor and the epistemological fallout this causes. The choice to live in the midst of the oppressor requires some form of engagement with the oppressor because it is almost impossible to avoid the structures of whiteness. These structures embody an ethos that shapes our physical and epistemological realities.

Throughout the novel, Jim constantly lives with the reality that he cannot avoid contact with the oppressor if he hopes to free the rest of his family. The power dynamic between oppressed and oppressor is always in play, even with those like Huck who are willing to help Jim. The temptation currently is to claim that this power dynamic has been diminished and the playing field is leveled. The idea of reconciliation is possible because African Americans and Euro-Americans can equally flourish in an environment together.

In Methodism, this idea of reconciliation usually moves toward discussions of reuniting the traditional African American Methodist denominations with the UMC.[34] The implication is that a stronger Methodist Church will be created that can move forward under one Methodist umbrella. Theologically, it could mean the Methodist Church is living out the eschatological future now by embodying the new creation. The problem is the UMC, which is a reflection of society, still embodies whiteness and would continue to do so if some form of a merger occurred. Moreover, the embodiment of whiteness is complicated, as I have attempted to demonstrate, because there will be those like Huck who will perpetuate whiteness, but who believe they are doing the right thing. Let me be clear it is not that they are doing the wrong thing but that they often misunderstand how the very structures of society and church perpetuate whiteness.

Reuniting the traditional African American denominations with the UMC is a mistake at this juncture because the power dynamics perpetuating whiteness are still in play. An example that really clarifies the perpetuation of whiteness is one of the assumptions of reconciliation. In general conversations with Euro-American students, pastors, and laity, the one statement they all make resembles this: "It would be great if the other denominations came back into the UMC." The assumption behind this statement is the traditional African American denominations would dismantle and be folded into the UMC—the predominantly Euro-American denomination. Not one of these individuals ever suggested that the UMC should dismantle and fold into one of the other denominations. Certainly one can cite various reasons the assumption is to fold the others into the UMC, but it is an assumption that has the effect of perpetuating whiteness.

The truth is, just like we must recognize the power dynamic inherent in Jim's relationship with Tom and Huck, if we are living out our Pan-Methodist salvation as God calls us to do, then we must also recognize the power dynamic inherent in reconciliation conversations. Most Euro-American United Methodists are interested in a form of reconciliation that, consciously or unconsciously, promotes just-us. Reconciling on this basis will not enhance flourishing and can diminish it to a greater extent. I am proposing that the goal for Methodists and for moving toward justice and not just-us needs to be reconsidered in light of our contextual situation. A more helpful initial step is what I term *engaging friendships*.

Engaging Friendships

Jim gives us a clue to what it means to be in an engaging friendship when he suggests friends do not shame one another.[35] The point is that friendship should enhance the chances of the other for flourishing, not diminish those chances. The challenge, given the power dynamic that exists in some relationships, is learning how to move toward an engaging friendship. In the novel *The Color Purple*, Alice Walker's main character, Celie, provides clues for developing such a friendship. Celie transforms a one-sided hierarchal relationship, where she had no power, into a relationship built on mutuality. Pan-Methodists and other fractured communities having power dynamics as a central concern can benefit from analyzing the process of transformation in Celie's relationships.

The power differential between Celie and Mr. ____ is evident from the very beginning of their relationship. Celie describes in vivid language how she is forced to display herself to Mr. ____, and how they become husband and wife.[36] The imagery of Mr. ____ up high on the horse and Celie far below him is indicative of the relationship between the two of them. Mr. ____ gets to decide whether Celie is suitable for him, and her voice at this point in the novel is silent.

What makes this scene even more horrid is the conscious reminder of slave auctions. Celie is made to go out on a stage and be checked out by Mr. ____ like he is purchasing an object. This is the same way traders often sold the slaves at auction. This scene not only points to gender oppression but also the ways in which some within the African American community mirrored the oppressive practices of Euro-Americans against other African Americans. Walker is very astute because she suggests an epistemological link between gender and racial oppression within the African American community. Some African American males, in trying to resolve the tension of being black in America, capitulate toward mirroring the practices of their oppressor in an effort to be American.

These men end up placing African American women in the same surrogate role as their Euro-American counterparts. Mr. ____ is interested in Celie for the purpose of taking care of his children.[37] There is no love interest or any hint at forming a mutual relationship; Mr. ____ simply needs a surrogate mother figure in the house. Delores Williams points out that Walker uses Celie and the other female characters to highlight "that the inordinate demands men make upon the nurturing capacities of black mothers are destructive."[38] I will add that these demands are destructive for the entire community because they reinforce not only gender oppression but also the oppressive practices of Euro-Americans against the black community. The fact that some African American males mirror the actions of their Euro-American counterparts illumines how pervasive an ethos of oppression can become within a community.

Celie reflects this pervasive ethos of oppression in her understanding of God. For Celie, God represents another level of male dominance that maintains an oppressive status quo. At one point in the novel, Celie tells Shug she does not write to God anymore because God is a man and no different from the other men she knows.[39] Celie is not able to distinguish between the actions of God and men at this point in her life, making the two almost synonymous. A part of Celie's transformation is reexamining some of her central understandings about God, men, and church.[40] This reexamination includes sexism within her own community and racial issues with the broader community. This transformation culminates in one of the classic lines from the novel by Celie, "I'm pore, I'm black, I may be ugly and can't cook, a voice say to everything listening. But I'm here."[41]

Celie's idea for what it means to be "here" is very powerful. It suggests an understanding of survival in the midst of an ethos of oppression, even though she is a poor black woman. The structures of oppression surrounding her may intensify her suffering, but because Celie is undergoing a transformation, she no longer views those structures as determinative. Surviving in the midst of an ethos of oppression means a new sense of empowerment that develops a different epistemological strategy that includes separation from the main cause of her suffering—Mr. ____. Because whiteness and sexism permeate the very structures of society, she cannot completely adjust her epistemological frame or live in isolation away from all men forever. Celie is able to understand how she can survive within those structures in such a manner that her life moves toward flourishing.

A significant part of her flourishing is when she starts sewing pants.[42] This seemingly innocuous act is the basis for her and Mr. ____ developing an engaging friendship. One day, while Celie is sewing, Mr. ____ tells her he used to sew with his mother until others laughed at him. Celie lays the groundwork for altering the relationship between her and Mr. ____ by deconstructing his understanding of sewing as feminine. Celie even agrees to teach him to sew.[43]

A transformation occurs in the relationship between Celie and Mr. ____ that no longer promotes an unhealthy power dynamic. The relationship is no longer one-sided, with Mr. ____ telling Celie how to live. Celie is the one who sets the rules of engagement for the relationship, which means the status quo has been altered. Mr. ____ starts sewing, which is perceived as a female activity and one that he stopped doing as a youth because others laughed at him. Because he seeks to establish an engaging friendship with Celie, he is willing to alter his understanding of what are male and female practices. Celie also is a participant in this process in her willingness to teach Mr. ____ how to sew.

Another transformation that occurs when Celie and Mr. ____ develop an engaging friendship is Mr. ____'s understanding of maleness. Mr. ____ believed that his role was to rule over Celie and use power abusively. Mr. ____'s perspective of maleness changes in the process of him and Celie developing an engaging friendship. Celie is so successful in changing Mr. ____'s perception of femininity and masculinity that he re-examines what it means to be male in society and alters his previous practices toward Celie.[44]

Interestingly, in the midst of Mr. ____'s transformation process he asks Celie to marry him again, but this time in the spirit and flesh.[45] Celie's response to Mr. ____ is no! She just wants to remain friends.[46] Celie is willing to develop an engaging friendship with Mr. ____, but she stops short of complete reconciliation. Celie's hesitation about complete reconciliation does not mean it is never appropriate; it does mean that reconciliation requires a lot deeper thought than we often give it. Maintaining an engaging friendship keeps Celie and Mr. ____ in relationship without some of the just-us power issues present previously. For example, Mr. ____'s awareness of his maleness is a result of developing an engaging friendship with Celie, in turn as a result of her empowerment. Reconciling does not mean Mr. ____'s awareness will end, but maintaining an engaging friendship guarantees Celie's empowerment because of her ability to set the rules for engagement.

Theologically, we can learn from this model some important insights regarding engaging friendships. I already outlined some of the gender insights in the above paragraphs and will move to the racial insights we can infer from this model. In his book *Intimacy & Mission*, Luther Smith outlines ways in which communities can begin to live intentionally with one another. I am adapting some of his ideas for what I am proposing is an engaging friendship. Admittedly, Smith is more willing to argue for reconciliation as an important Christian goal than I am, but I think my adaptation is still fair to his overall concerns.

Smith uses the language of being in fellowship with companions.[47] The language itself points toward a deeper sense of friendship between various entities. What Smith seeks to capture is the "intentional and intense commitment" required for constructing community.[48] This is not a commitment for getting just one's agenda accomplished or just one's issues addressed, but a commitment to seeing and listening to the other. If the power dynamic is one-sided, then it is not possible to have an intentional and intense commitment to a relationship. Mr. ____ was not committed to being in relationship with Celie until the power dynamic was altered. As long as the terms of the relationship favor one party over the other, no impetus exists for the one in power to commit to a relationship of mutuality. Seeking a relationship based upon mutuality requires moving beyond just-us concerns to "laboring on behalf of God's justice and love."[49] It is when Mr. ____ experiences a transformation in his life that he can really see and hear Celie for the first time. This transformation occurs because she is able to set the rules for engagement.

An engaging friendship requires modeling God's justice and love in a manner that enhances the chances of another flourishing. The challenge many Euro-Americans face is that love of self too often becomes another means for loving whiteness. Many Euro-Americans need a transformation similar to the one Mr.____ experienced when he confronted his maleness. In the process of this transformation, the ability to see and listen to another will also be transformed. Opportunities for forming intentional and intense relationships that are based upon mutuality will occur.

These opportunities can also lead to what Smith terms "prophetic neighboring." Smith writes, "*Prophetic neighboring* occurs from caring relationship. A congregation need not wait for a catastrophe to happen before it relates with neighbors. To wait would suggest that neighboring is only a response to someone's problems or weakness. A caring neighbor seeks to be in relationship because the relationship itself is valued."[50] The key phrase is "the relationship itself is valued." Celie and Mr. ____ get to a point in their friendship where the relationship itself is valued. The two of them would sit on the porch sewing and talking with each other—the relationship is valuable.

Engaging friendships require valuing the relationship itself. All parties involved have to do this. The former oppressor cannot enter the relationship with the hopes of returning things to the status quo, and those formerly experiencing oppression cannot enter the relationship simply for some form of gain—be it economic or related to status. An engaging friendship is based upon valuing the friendship itself and caring for one's friend. It is this understanding of friendship that gets us closer to a love of neighbor that models God's justice and not just our own interest.

Smith suggests if we are committed to community and embody prophetic neighboring, then we will actually live into God's promise for us.[51] This does not mean life is perfect or that various challenges to the relationship will not occur, but it does mean we are called to live out God's promise for community on this side of salvation.[52] Ultimately it is God's intent for all things to be reconciled, and this is why reconciliation is a very important Christian concept. I am proposing a penultimate hope that eventually can lead to reconciliation—engaging friendships. The wisdom of Celie in not completely reconciling with Mr. ____ and maintaining an engaging friendship with him is a model that can aid race relations, not only among Pan-Methodists but among other fractured groups as well.

The advantage of starting with an engaging friendship is that it takes seriously the power dynamic that exists in relationships. Because the parties do not completely reconcile, the party who experienced oppression retains the space to determine the terms of the friendship. The terms between Celie and Mr. ____ were to sew together on the porch. Obviously the terms will differ depending on the context of the parties involved, but those who experienced the oppression have to set the terms. This does not mean complete reconciliation will never occur, but it does mean it will be entered into with deep consideration.

Pan-Methodist Implications

This model has several implications for Pan-Methodists and other fractured groups. First, developing an engaging friendship takes the pressure off of reconciliation considerations. Thinking in terms of an engaging friendship shifts the conversation between entities away from concerns related to reconciliation toward deepening what it means to value friendship itself. One of the challenges with reconciliation considerations is power—who keeps it and who loses it. If the focus is on an engaging friendship, then the issue of power is not as critical. For example, any reconciliation talks among Pan-Methodists would have to resolve the issue of which bishops from the various denominations continue in their current position and which ones do not. This is a conversation that is riddled with power issues that quickly can move into just-us concerns. The reality is each denomination would attempt to protect its bishops' territory. A shift to developing an engaging friendship that permeates the culture of all the denominations has a better chance of challenging just-us concerns because it redefines structural commitments.

Second, developing an engaging friendship focuses on modeling God's justice and love. This is not to say that reconciliation considerations do not have this focus, but the emphasis of an engaging friendship model is on mirroring God's justice and love. For Pan-Methodists, this means developing relationships at the local church level, at the episcopal level, and even within academic circles. These relationships need to be intentional and committed to moving beyond just-us concerns to how we as Pan-Methodists can embody the justice of Jesus. This will require a risk of faith at all levels and a commitment to being in community. The challenge for those within the predominantly Euro-American United Methodist Church will be understanding that they cannot set the agenda for the friendship. The challenge for those in the predominantly African American denominations will be understanding that the agenda has to be set in such a way that we are modeling God's justice and love.

Finally, developing an engaging friendship means seeking opportunities to practice justice within the broader community. Interestingly, the pants Celie and Mr.____ sewed together benefited many within the broader community. Their focus was not simply inward but also looked out toward others. Those within the Pan-Methodist family have to find ways to look out toward others while transformation occurs within the family. This is especially important at the local congregation level, where opportunities to partner together in a way that a community can be transformed are important. Developing this type of partnership can only deepen the friendship experienced between congregations.

My hope is that moving toward a Pan-Methodist soteriology will give congregations a means of embodying a love of neighbor based upon the other flourishing. Sondra Matthaei has a similar vision for UMC congregations that can be broadened to the entire Pan-Methodist family. She writes:

> I have a vision of the church as the body of Christ living as a communion of grace, a sign of the reign of God already present in this life. But it is only with manifest trust in God's grace working in the church through the Holy Spirit that I have dared to propose the hopeful vision in this book, a vision of a communion of grace. In this communion, the church, with God's help, tries to live as the body of Christ in the interdependence of mutual indwelling and in the acceptance of diversity through room-giving.[53]

I am suggesting for Pan-Methodists that interdependent mutual indwelling can happen if engaging friendships are formed that embody the lived reality of all Methodist traditions. This is a vision that reexamines our preconceived ideas about our neighbors and challenges us not only to dialogue with one another about God's justice and love but to embody it.

Conclusion

I have argued in the preceding chapters that the way we perceive soteriology often promotes just-us and not justice. For Pan-Methodists, because of the different splinter denominations, the just-us gets magnified, as all of the denominations are comfortable staying on their side of the fence. It is my hope that we can create a neighborhood where the fences are lowered and dialogue can begin at all levels of the church. The purpose of this dialogue is not to move toward reconciling into one denomination but to develop engaging friendships. For this vision to become a reality, more work has to be done in two areas.

First, the term *Methodism* in many circles has become synonymous with United Methodism and promotes Wesleyan thinking that often excludes the broader Pan-Methodist family. For example, Methodist studies really means a focus on Wesleyan studies and the implications for The United Methodist Church. The African American Methodist denominations are usually only given a cursory overview or skipped altogether. I have attempted to expose the fallacy in this line of thinking by arguing for a more inclusive understanding of Methodism. I am not suggesting that the Wesleyan heritage is unimportant, because I am also an integral part of that heritage, but I am suggesting that Methodism in the United States has to include the lived reality and thinking of African Americans. If Methodism continues to be synonymous with a particular way of thinking, then the term itself represents just-us. Moving toward a Pan-Methodist soteriology is an attempt to reclaim the broader meaning of Methodism in this context.

Second, the Pan-Methodist family has to find ways to build engaging friendships. Conducting annual choir and pulpit exchanges cannot develop these friendships. I am not downplaying the importance of the exchanges but simply pointing out that the exchanges are a first step and not a long-term answer to developing lasting relationships. Engaging friendships are developed when communities are intentional about dialoguing together on an ongoing basis. For example, Bible studies that involve at least two different Pan-Methodist communities and shared youth activities are just a couple of examples of making steps toward a more long-term engaging friendship. The central point is finding ways to create an ongoing dialogue that at times may be painful, but with God's grace is also transforming.

One book will not achieve the goals I highlighted above, but it is my hope that a conversation will ensue that considers what we mean by the term *Methodist* and how we can foster engaging friendships. If we are willing to take the risk of faith, as Jesus did, to embody God's justice and love, then our relationship with our neighbors will be transformed. This is not an easy task because all parties involved are more comfortable sitting on their side of the fence. Lowering the fence or removing it altogether is not comfortable because the other is now within view and cannot be ignored.

It is time we live with discomfort within Methodism by taking our neighbors seriously and moving toward an engaging friendship. The goal is to develop an engaging friendship that moves beyond politeness by looking at the power dynamics between the different denominations, both historically and currently. Moreover, the goal is to develop an engaging friendship that creates among churches, leaders, and academia, partnerships that embody God's justice and love to others. These types of friendships will not occur overnight, but it is my hope that thirty years from now we will not be having the same conversation. It is time that the Methodist Church reclaim its Pan-Methodist roots as it moves forward to embody God's reign.

NOTES

Introduction

1. James Cone and Jacquelyn Grant are two figures within the AME tradition who have influenced my thinking. Historically, Frederick Douglass and Sojourner Truth have been important figures in the AMEZ tradition and they continue to influence my thinking. William McClain and Rosetta Ross are two African American figures within the UMC who have had an influence on my thinking. Within the CME tradition Evelyn Parker and Luther Smith Jr. are figures who influence my thinking. My point is that the broader Methodist tradition has been shaped by both men and women thinkers.

2. By *Pan-Methodist* I mean a theology that reflects the perspective of the traditional African American Methodist Churches and blacks in The United Methodist Church in conversation with the predominately Euro-American United Methodist Church. I am arguing for a movement toward a Pan-Methodist theological perspective because the voices of womanists, Latinos and Hispanics, Native Americans, and Korean Americans are not prominently featured in this book.

3. Richard Pryor would at times use this term in his comedy act as a throwaway line, but I think it appropriately describes what can happen to communities at times when they become entrenched in their own issues. For example, individuals who do not want landfills in their neighborhood often ignore the fact that the landfill that gets placed in an economically disadvantaged neighborhood.

4. Dennis C. Dickerson, *Religion, Race, and Region: Research Notes on A.M.E. Church History* (Nashville: AMEC Sunday School Union, 1995), 17.

5. James Thomas, *Methodism's Racial Dilemma* (Nashville: Abingdon Press, 1992), 39–40.

6. Ibid., 131.

7. The pastor has asked to remain anonymous.

1. Historical Roots of Just-us

1. Lewis V. Baldwin, "Early African American Methodism: Founders and Foundations," in *Heritage and Hope: The African-American Presence in United Methodism*, ed. Grant S. Shockley (Nashville: Abingdon Press, 1991), 24.

2. Frederick Norwood, *The Story of American Methodism* (Nashville: Abingdon Press, 1974), 186.

3. Othal Hawthorne Lakey, *The History of the CME Church*, rev. ed. (Memphis: General Board of Publications, CME Church, 1997), 47.

4. Ibid., 77.

5. Ibid., 87.

6. Ibid.

7. Harry Richardson, *Dark Salvation: The Story of Methodism as It Developed among Blacks in America* (New York: Doubleday, 1976), 39.

8. Although some sociologists like E. Franklin Frazier and W. E. B. DuBois question the retention of traditional African elements in the religious practices of slaves in America, others like Melvin Herskovits suggest otherwise.

9. Lakey, *History of the CME Church*, 98.

10. Ibid., 96.

11. Ibid.
12. Norwood, *Story of American Methodism*, 186.
13. Lakey, *History of the CME Church*, 96.
14. Ibid., 97.
15. Norwood, *Story of American Methodism*, 201.
16. Ibid., 201–2.
17. Richard Allen, *The Life Experience and Gospel Labors of the Rt. Rev. Richard Allen* (Nashville: Abingdon Press, 1960; Bicentennial Edition, 1983), 25.
18. Will Gravely, "Reassessing the African American Presence in Early Methodism in the United States, 1769–1809," in *Methodism and the Shaping of American Culture*, eds. Nathan O. Hatch and John H. Wigger (Nashville: Abingdon Press, 2001), 183.
19. William Gravely, *Gilbert Haven, Methodist Abolitionist: A Study in Race, Religion, and Reform, 1850–1880* (Nashville: Abingdon Press, 1973), 182.
20. Ibid.
21. Gravely, "Reassessing the African American Presence in Early Methodism," 184.
22. Allen, *Rt. Rev. Richard Allen*, 22–23.
23. Gravely, "Reassessing the African American Presence in Early Methodism," 187.
24. Ibid., 192.
25. James M. McPherson, *The Struggle for Equality: Abolitionists and the Negro in the Civil War and Reconstruction* (Princeton, N.J.: Princeton University Press, 1964), 134.
26. Frederick Douglass, "The Claims of the Negro Ethnologically Considered," in *The Life and Writings of Frederick Douglass*, vol. 2, ed. Philip S. Foner (New York: International Publishers, 1950), 295. Frederick Douglass was a member of the AMEZ Church and one of the foremost statesmen and abolitionists in the United States.
27. David Walker, *David Walker's Appeal to the Coloured Citizens of the World*, ed. Peter P. Hinks (University Park: Pennsylvania State University Press, original publication 1829, third printing 2003), 30. David Walker was an African American Methodist living in Boston who wrote one of the most controversial books during the early 1800s.
28. Thomas Jefferson, *Notes on the State of Virginia*, ed. David Waldstreicher (New York: Palgrave, 2002), 180. This quote also appears in *Walker's Appeal* on pages xxvi and xxvii.
29. Walker, *Appeal*, 35–36.
30. Jefferson, *Notes on the State of Virginia*, 176.
31. Douglass, "Claims of the Negro," 299.
32. Ibid.
33. Ibid.
34. Ibid.
35. Gravely, *Gilbert Haven*, 179.
36. Gilbert Haven, "National Sermons: Sermons, Speeches and Letters on Slavery and Its War," in *The Anti-Slavery Crusade in America* (New York: Arno Press, 1969), 624.
37. Gravely, *Gilbert Haven*, 180.
38. Ibid., 180–81.
39. Ibid.
40. Ibid., 184–85.
41. Ibid., 190.
42. Ibid., 171.
43. Ibid., 181.
44. Haven, "National Sermons," 622.
45. John H. Wigger, *Taking Heaven by Storm: Methodism and the Rise of Popular Christianity in America* (Chicago and Urbana: University of Illinois Press, 2001), 180.
46. This is John Wigger's thesis in his book *Taking Heaven by Storm*.
47. Ibid., 185.
48. Lakey, *History of the CME Church*, 77–78.

49. John Wesley, preface to "Hymns and Sacred Poems," *The Works of John Wesley* (Grand Rapids, Mich.: Zondervan, 1959), 14:321.

50. Phoebe Palmer, *Phoebe Palmer Selected Writings*, ed. Thomas Oden (New York: Paulist Press, 1988), 13.

51. Ibid., 11.

52. Read the biographies of Jarena Lee or Julia Foote to find similar patterns in the meetings where they preached. *Sisters of the Spirit*, ed. William L. Andrews (Bloomington: Indiana University Press, 1986).

53. Cheryl Townsend Gilkes, *If It Wasn't for the Women: Black Women's Experience and Womanist Culture in Church and Community* (Maryknoll, N.Y.: Orbis Books, 2001), 20.

54. Maria Stewart, "What If I Am a Woman?," in *Let Nobody Turn Us Around: Voices of Resistance, Reform, and Renewal*, eds. Manning Marable and Leith Mullings (Lanham, Md.: Rowman & Littlefield, 2000), 44.

55. Donald G. Mathews, *Slavery and Methodism: A Chapter in American Morality, 1780–1845* (Princeton, N.J.: Princeton University Press, 1965), 88.

56. Nathan Bangs, *History of the Methodist Episcopal Church*, vol. 4 (New York: G. Lane and P. P. Sandford, 1841), 111.

57. Ibid., 45–46.

58. Walker, *Appeal*, 48–49.

59. Nathan Bangs, "The American Colonization Society," *Methodist Magazine and Quarterly Review* XV (January 1833): 111–16. See also Mathews, *Slavery and Methodism*, 102.

2. Experiencing Just-us

1. Randy L. Maddox, "The Enriching Role of Experience," in *Wesley and the Quadrilateral: Renewing the Conversation*, ed. W. Stephen Gunter et al. (Nashville: Abingdon Press, 1997), 108.

2. Ibid.

3. Ibid.

4. John Wesley, Sermon XI, "The Witness of the Spirit II," *The Works of John Wesley*, vol. 1 (Nashville: Abingdon Press, 1984), IV.1.

5. Randy L. Maddox, *Responsible Grace: John Wesley's Practical Theology* (Nashville: Kingswood Books, 1994), 46.

6. Theodore Runyon, *The New Creation: John Wesley's Theology Today* (Nashville: Abingdon Press, 1998), 154–56.

7. See Colossians 3:1-17.

8. Runyon, *New Creation*, 146.

9. Ibid., 160.

10. Scott J. Jones, *John Wesley's Conception and Use of Scripture* (Nashville: Kingswood Books, 1995), 182.

11. Kelly Brown Douglas, *The Black Christ* (Maryknoll, N.Y.: Orbis Books, 1994), 15.

12. James H. Cone, *God of the Oppressed* (New York: Seabury Press, 1975), 8.

13. Ibid., 3.

14. I am using the theme of liberation, but other themes such as survival also could be used as a lens for thinking about the African American experience. Delores Williams has done the most work around this theme in her book *Sisters in the Wilderness: The Challenge of Womanist God-talk* (Maryknoll, N.Y.: Orbis Books, 1993).

15. Paraphrase of 1 John 4:20-21.

16. Cone, *God of the Oppressed*, 33.

17. James H. Cone, *For My People* (Maryknoll, N.Y.: Orbis Books, 1996), 13–14.

18. Jacquelyn Grant, *White Women's Christ and Black Women's Jesus: Feminist Christology and Womanist Response* (Atlanta: Scholars Press, 1989), 11.

19. I purposely use the language of the Methodist tradition because this means African American and Wesleyan sources are valid resources.

20. Sallie McFague, *The Body of God: An Ecological Theology* (Minneapolis: Fortress Press, 1993), 48–49.

21. Ibid., 49–50.

22. Renita Weems, "Womanist Reflections on Biblical Hermeneutics," in *Black Theology*, vol. 2, eds. James H. Cone and Gayraud Wilmore (Maryknoll, N.Y.: Orbis Books, 1993), 216.

23. Rebekah Miles, "The Faith behind the Confession: Postmodern Assumptions behind the United Methodist Confessing Movement," in *Quarterly Review* (winter 1997–98): 351.

24. Sojourner Truth, "Ain't I a Woman?" in *Let Nobody Turn Us Around: Voices of Resistance, Reform, and Renewal*, eds. Manning Marble and Leith Mullings (Lanham, Md.: Rowan & Littlefield, 2000), 68.

25. Ibid.

26. Ibid.

27. Laceye Warner, "Saving Women: Re-visioning Contemporary Concepts of Evangelism," in *Considering the Great Commission: Evangelism and Mission in the Wesleyan Spirit*, eds. Stephen Gunter and Elaine Robinson (Nashville: Abingdon Press, 2005), 130.

28. Ibid., 131.

29. Grant, *White Women's Christ and Black Women's Jesus*, 215.

30. Warner, "Saving Women," 131–32

31. Jacquelyn Grant, "Womanist Theology: Black Women's Experience as a Source for Doing Theology, with Special Reference to Christology," in *Black Theology*, vol. 2, 284.

32. Rebekah Miles, "The Faith behind the Confession: Postmodern Assumptions behind the United Methodist Confession Movement," *Quarterly Review* (winter 1997–98): 351.

3. Wesleyan Soteriological Just-us

1. I use the language of *via salutis* (versus *ordo salutis*) because it has become more prominent in Wesleyan thought.

2. John Wesley, Sermon 43, "The Scripture Way of Salvation," *The Works of John Wesley*, vol. 2 (Nashville: Abingdon Press, 1985), I.3.

3. Wesley, Sermon 45, "The New Birth," *Works*, 1.

4. Wesley, "The Scripture Way of Salvation," I.4.

5. Ibid.

6. Randy L. Maddox, *Responsible Grace: John Wesley's Practical Theology* (Nashville: Kingswood Books, 1994), 69.

7. Wesley, "The Scripture Way of Salvation," I.4.

8. *Wesley and the Quadrilateral: Renewing the Conversation*, ed. Stephen Gunter, et al. Stephen Gunter in chapter 1 makes an argument for reading Wesley as a thinker within his context.

9. Kenneth J. Collins, "Conversion in the Wesleyan Tradition," in *Conversion in the Wesleyan Tradition*, eds. Kenneth J. Collins and John H. Tyson (Nashville: Abingdon Press, 2001), 18.

10. Ibid.

11. Ibid., 12.

12. John H. Tyson, "John Wesley's Conversion at Aldersgate," in *Conversion in the Wesleyan Tradition*, 37.

13. Ibid., 31.

14. Ibid., 32.

15. Kenneth J. Collins, "Real Christianity as an Integrating Theme in Wesley's Soteriology: The Critique of a Modern Myth," in *Asbury Theological Journal* 51, no. 2 (fall 1996): 26.

16. Tyson, "John Wesley's Conversion," 36.

17. Collins, "Real Christianity," 26.

18. Tyson, "John Wesley's Conversion," 36.

19. Ibid., 32–33.
20. Please note the articles by Estrelda Alexander and Doug Strong in *Conversion in the Wesleyan Tradition*. I am not claiming these authors are solely within the conversion school of thought, but that their projects were written within a conversion context about Methodism.
21. Tyson, "John Wesley's Conversion," 31–32.
22. Maddox, *Responsible Grace*, 158.
23. Ibid., 159.
24. Ibid., 19.
25. Ibid.
26. Ibid.
27. Ibid., 159.
28. Ibid.
29. Ibid., 152.
30. Ibid.
31. Ibid.
32. Ibid.
33. This is not a critique against conversionists, but rather the issue is pushing a conversionist position to the extreme.
34. Maddox, *Responsible Grace*, 141.
35. Ibid.
36. Ibid., 145.
37. Theodore Runyon, *The New Creation: John Wesley's Theology Today* (Nashville: Abingdon Press, 1998), 57.
38. Ibid.
39. Ibid., 57–58.
40. Ibid., 12.
41. Ibid., 8.
42. John Wesley, "The General Spread of the Gospel," *Works*, 2:499.
43. Runyon, *New Creation*, 229.
44. Ibid., 17.
45. Ibid., 22.
46. Ibid.
47. Ibid., 202.
48. Ibid.
49. Ibid., 169–70.
50. Ibid., 231.
51. James Cone, *The Risks of Faith* (Boston: Beacon Press, 1999), 138.
52. Susie C. Stanley, "Sanctified Feminism," in *Quarterly Review* (winter 2003): 386–87.
53. Catherine Keller, "Salvation Flows: Eschatology for a Feminist Wesleyanism," in *Quarterly Review* (winter 2003): 413.
54. Ibid., 414.
55. Ibid.
56. Ibid.
57. Ibid., 422.
58. Ibid.
59. Stanley, "Sanctified Feminism," 392–93.
60. Ibid., 393.
61. To be fair, Warner's emphasis is evangelism, but soteriological issues are intertwined in her evangelistic discussions.
62. Laceye C. Warner, *Saving Women: Retrieving Evangelistic Theology and Practice* (Waco, Tex.: Baylor Press, 2007), 117–24.

63. Ibid., 112–13.

64. Ibid., 139.

65. Ibid., 280.

66. I focus my critique on Warner because her work really moves us in the right direction. In some ways critiquing the others would be easier but probably not as insightful as thinking about reconciliation at a deeper level.

67. Warner, *Saving Women*, 276.

68. James H. Cone, *A Black Theology of Liberation: Twentieth Anniversary Edition* (Maryknoll, N.Y.: Orbis Books, 1990), 86.

69. Ibid., 85.

4. African American Soteriological Just-us

1. Albert J. Raboteau, *Slave Religion: The "Invisible Institution" in the Antebellum South* (New York: Oxford University Press, 1978), 4.

2. Ibid., 145–46.

3. Ibid., 132.

4. C. Eric Lincoln and Lawrence H. Mamiya, *The Black Church in the African American Experience* (Durham, N.C.: Duke University Press, 1990), 4.

5. Ibid., 5.

6. DuBois coins this term in his seminal work, *The Souls of Black Folk*, in *The Oxford W. E. B. DuBois Reader*, ed. Eric J. Sundquist (New York: Oxford University Press, 1996), 102. This idea of double consciousness is intensified for African American women who are trying to flourish in an androcentric environment along with the other forms of oppression.

7. James H. Cone, *A Black Theology of Liberation: Twentieth Anniversary Edition* (Maryknoll, N.Y.: Orbis Books, 1990), 45.

8. Ibid., 140.

9. Ibid., 141.

10. Ibid., 137.

11. Ibid., 141.

12. James H. Cone, *God of the Oppressed* (New York: Seabury Press, 1975), 152.

13. Cone, *Black Theology*, 2.

14. Ibid., 3.

15. See chapter 3 of Schubert M. Ogden's *Faith and Freedom: Toward a Theology of Liberation* (Nashville: Abingdon Press, 1979), in which Ogden argues that liberation theologies do a poor job of delineating between God's work of redemption and God's work of emancipation.

16. Ibid., 71.

17. Cone, *Black Theology*, 3.

18. Ogden, *Faith and Freedom*, 71–73.

19. Cone, *God of the Oppressed*, 118–19.

20. Ibid., 115–16.

21. "O Freedom," in *Songs of Zion* (Nashville: Abingdon Press, 1981), 102–3.

22. Cone, *God of the Oppressed*, 113.

23. J. Deotis Roberts, *Liberation and Reconciliation: A Black Theology* (Maryknoll, N.Y.: Orbis Books, 1994), 9.

24. Ibid., 58.

25. Ibid.

26. Ibid., 59.

27. Certainly some individuals will point to the Truth and Reconciliation Commission as a model for collective forgiveness, but I think the jury is still out on the effectiveness of that model in relation to the oppressed.

28. Roberts, *Liberation and Reconciliation*, 60.
29. Ibid., 60–61.
30. Ibid., 73.
31. Ibid., 74.
32. Ibid., 81.
33. Ibid., 7.
34. Ibid., 95.
35. Ibid.
36. Ibid.
37. Cone, *God of the Oppressed*, 240.
38. Delores S. Williams, *Sisters in the Wilderness: The Challenge of Womanist God-Talk* (Maryknoll, N.Y.: Orbis Books, 1993), 1–2.
39. Ibid., 15.
40. Ibid., 15–33.
41. Ibid., 33.
42. Ibid., 144.
43. Ibid., 151.
44. Ibid., 116–17.
45. Ibid., 116.
46. Ibid., 113.
47. Ibid.
48. Ibid., 116.
49. Ibid., 113.
50. Ibid., 117.
51. Ibid.
52. Ibid., 139. The women Williams describes were active in the struggle for equality during the Civil Rights era.
53. Ibid., 165.
54. Ibid., 164.
55. Ibid., 165.
56. Ibid.
57. Ibid.

5. *Moving toward a Pan-Methodist Soteriology*

1. Sallie McFague, *The Body of God: An Ecological Theology* (Minneapolis: Fortress Press, 1993), 164.
2. Ibid., 36–37.
3. J. Kameron Carter, "Repetition, or the Theological Failures of Modern Dignity Discourse: The Case of Frederick Douglass's 1845 *Narrative*," in *God and Human Dignity*, eds. R. Kendall Soulen and Linda Woodhead (Grand Rapids, Mich.: Eerdmans, 2006), 215.
4. John B. Cobb Jr., *Postmodernism and Public Policy: Reframing Religion, Culture, Education, Sexuality, Class, Race, Politics, and the Economy* (Albany: State University of New York Press, 2002), 155.
5. Karen Baker-Fletcher, *Dancing with God: The Trinity from a Womanist Perspective* (St. Louis: Chalice Press, 2006), 129.
6. Kenneth J. Collins, *The Theology of John Wesley: Holy Love and the Shape of Grace* (Nashville: Abingdon Press, 2007), 74.
7. Baker-Fletcher, *Dancing with God*, 161.
8. Ibid.
9. Ibid., 142.
10. Ibid.

11. Jacquelyn Grant, *White Women's Christ and Black Women's Jesus: Feminist Christology and Womanist Response* (Atlanta: Scholars Press, 1989), 219.
12. Cobb, *Postmodernism and Public Policy*, 150.
13. James H. Cone, *God of the Oppressed* (New York: Seabury Press, 1975), 138.
14. Cobb, *Postmodernism and Public Policy*, 160.
15. Ibid., 156.
16. I am not claiming Collins is a traditionalist but that his reading of Wesley fits within a more traditional understanding of justification.
17. Collins, *Theology of John Wesley*, 167.
18. Ibid.
19. Ibid.
20. Baker-Fletcher, *Dancing with God*, 161.
21. Cone, *God of the Oppressed*, 141–42.
22. Collins, *Theology of John Wesley*, 230.
23. Baker-Fletcher, *Dancing with God*, 157.
24. Ibid., 157–58.
25. Ibid., 158.
26. Ibid., 159.
27. Theodore Runyon, *The New Creation: John Wesley's Theology Today* (Nashville: Abingdon Press, 1998), 225.
28. Ibid.
29. I am not claiming Runyon is arguing for hierarchal forms of love, but because Wesley emphasizes the divinity of Christ and downplays the humanity of Jesus, it is important to make explicit the difference in a Pan-Methodist approach.
30. Cobb, *Postmodernism and Public Policy*, 162.
31. Runyon, *New Creation*, 202.
32. Baker-Fletcher, *Dancing with God*, 161.

6. *Engaging Friendship*

1. Aristotle describes varying degrees of friendship and the basis for true friendship between equals. Aristotle, *Nicomachaen Ethics*, trans. Martin Ostwald (Indianapolis: Bobbs-Merrill, 1962).
2. Mark Twain, *The Adventures of Tom Sawyer* and *The Adventures of Huckleberry Finn* (New York: Random House, 1918), 277.
3. James H. Cone, *God of the Oppressed* (New York: Seabury Press, 1975), 238.
4. Twain uses the term *nigger* often in the novel in an attempt to maintain the speech of those during the time frame of the novel. In actual quotes I will stick with Twain's original text because it reinforces the point of power, but I will change the language in my analysis of the text.
5. Twain, *Huckleberry Finn*, 284–85.
6. Cone, *God of the Oppressed*, 238.
7. Twain, *Huckleberry Finn*, 285.
8. Ibid., 540.
9. Cone, *God of the Oppressed*, 241.
10. Tom is pretending to be Sid while Huck is pretending to be Tom at this point in the novel. So when he references Tom, he really means Huck.
11. Twain, *Huckleberry Finn*, 586.
12. Karen Baker-Fletcher, *Dancing with God: The Trinity from a Womanist Perspective* (St. Louis: Chalice Press, 2006), 93.
13. Cone, *God of the Oppressed*, 146.
14. Ibid., 147.
15. Ibid.

16. Twain, *Huckleberry Finn*, 357.
17. Ibid.
18. Ibid., 354.
19. Ibid.
20. Ibid.
21. Baker-Fletcher, *Dancing with God*, 115.
22. Ibid.
23. Twain, *Huckleberry Finn*, 581.
24. Ibid., 358–60.
25. Cone, *God of the Oppressed*, 242.
26. Luther Smith, *Intimacy & Mission: Intentional Community as Crucible for Radical Discipleship* (Scottdale, Pa.: Herald Press, 1994), 150.
27. It is important to note this reality is intensified for African American women, who also struggle with androcentrism in the United States.
28. Twain, *Huckleberry Finn*, 303–4.
29. Delores S. Williams, *Sisters in the Wilderness: The Challenge of Womanist God-talk* (Maryknoll, N.Y.: Orbis Books, 1993), 117.
30. I am not suggesting Jim faced the same uncertainty as Hagar, but the wilderness was a place where all slaves encountered possibility and danger.
31. Twain, *Huckleberry Finn*, 357.
32. Cone, *God of the Oppressed*, 147.
33. Ibid.
34. The traditional African American denominations are physically separated from the UMC but still live in a society that is structured to perpetuate whiteness. They still experience the balancing act of creating their own sacred space while living with the reality of a society that (dis)ables their complete flourishing.
35. Twain, *Huckleberry Finn*, 354.
36. Alice Walker, *The Color Purple* (New York: Pocket Books, 1982), 11–12.
37. Ibid., 8.
38. Williams, *Sisters in the Wilderness*, 53.
39. Walker, *Color Purple*, 199.
40. Williams, *Sisters in the Wilderness*, 53.
41. Walker, *Color Purple*, 214.
42. Ibid., 218–19.
43. Ibid., 279.
44. Ibid., 267.
45. Ibid., 290.
46. Ibid.
47. Smith, *Intimacy & Mission*, 78.
48. Ibid.
49. Ibid.
50. Ibid., 156.
51. Ibid., 161.
52. Ibid.
53. Sondra Matthaei, *Formation in Faith: The Congregational Ministry of Making Disciples* (Nashville: Abingdon Press, 2008), 94.

Made in the USA
San Bernardino, CA
05 January 2017